BBC Books, an imprint of Ebury Publishing
20 Vauxhall Bridge Road, London SW1V 2SA
BBC Books is part of the Penguin Random House group of companies
whose addresses can be found at global.penguinrandomhouse.com

Penguin
Random House
UK

This book is published to accompany the television series *Strictly Come Dancing*
first broadcast on BBC One in 2021.

Executive Producer: Sarah James
Series Director: Nikki Parsons
Series Producer: Jack Gledhill

With thanks to: Harriet Frost, Eve Winstanley, Joe Turner, Stefania Aleksander and Victoria Dalton.

First published by BBC Books in 2021
www.penguin.co.uk

A CIP catalogue record for this book is available from the British Library.

ISBN 9781785947643

Printed and bound in Italy by Elcograf S.p.A

Picture credits: BBC/Ray Burmiston: 6, 10, 12, 18, 20, 22, 28, 30, 34, 36, 38, 42, 44, 46, 52, 54, 58, 60, 66, 68, 70, 72, 74, 76, 82, 84, 86, 88, 90, 96, 98, 102, 104, 106, 108, 110, 116, 118, 120, 122 and 124. BBC/Guy Levy: 8, 24–27, 40–41, 48–51, 62–65, 79–81, 92–95 and 112–115.

ANNUAL

BOOKS

Contents

MEET THE PRO DANCERS

STRICTLY FEATURES

FUN AND TRIVIA

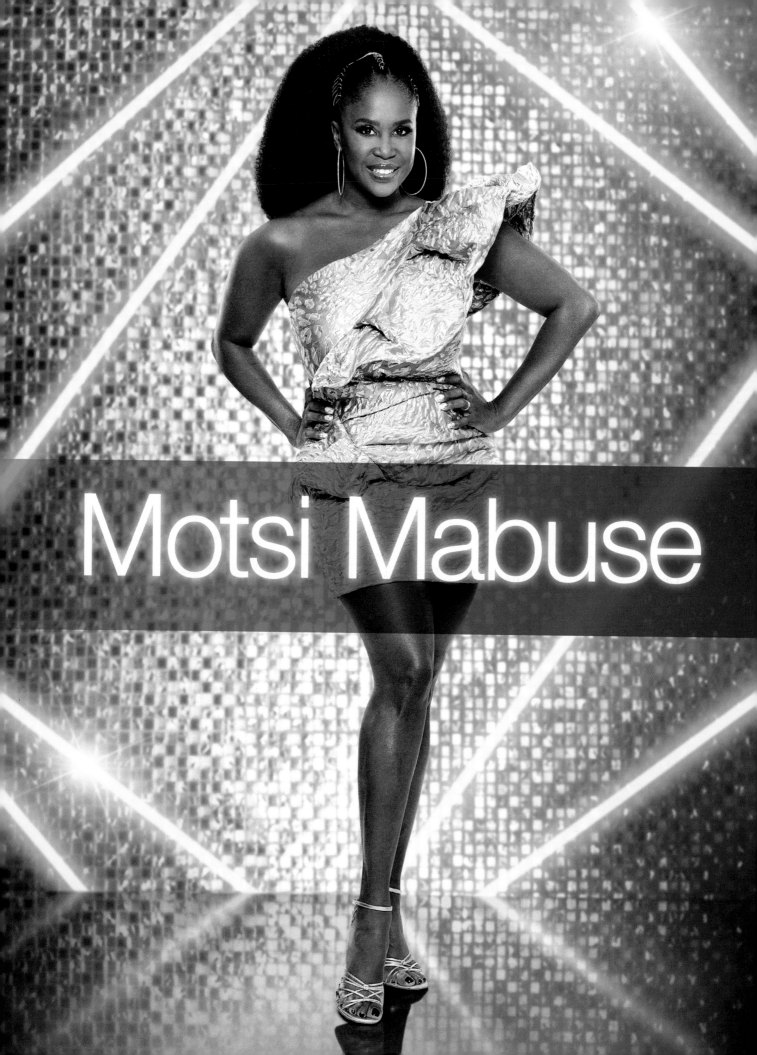

Motsi Mabuse

Motsi Mabuse is brimming over with excitement for her third series on the judges' panel. And she is looking forward to working alongside new judge Anton Du Beke.

'I'm excited to do the series and I'm looking forward to seeing everybody again,' she says. 'I'm really excited about the new combination of the judges. Everyone has seen Anton dancing for so many years and we're all so happy for him. It feels like destiny, and I can't wait to see what's going to happen – what is going to be the dynamic between the judges? I'm excited for the banter and the fun.

'It's always a delight to be part of *Strictly*, and this year I feel like I've finally settled in. Everybody's finding their groove again and it will be wonderful to be back.'

The former German Latin champ, who started her own dance career in her native South Africa, has been eyeing up the new talent for this series.

'The cast this year is brilliant because there's a lot of people from different areas of life and a lot of different personalities,' she says. 'It's really diverse, so it's going to be an exciting series. As soon as I know who's doing *Strictly*, I begin searching online, looking into everybody and wondering how they will do.

'I saw some videos of Rhys Stephenson and he looks like he could move well, and Tilly Ramsay too. Also, being in a boyband, Tom Fletcher is really popular and I think John Whaite could prove quite a mover, too.

'Adam Peaty signing up is so inspiring. Going through the pressure of the Olympics and then going straight on to do *Strictly* is incredible. He has the experience of being the best at something, so now he can go with the same ambitions for the *Strictly* glitterball.'

Ever enthusiastic, Motsi says she was overwhelmed by the series 18 Final and was delighted to see Bill Bailey lift the coveted trophy.

'I'm a big fan of HRVY and Jamie Laing, and Maisie Smith was unbelievable, but Bill was the right person at the right time,' she says. 'When he did that iconic dance to 'The Show Must Go On', I had to stop the tears because it was such a moving moment for me and for everyone at home.'

As a professional dancer and then a judge on the German version of the show, *Let's Dance*, before joining the *Strictly* panel, Motsi has seen both sides of the competition – and she has some sage advice for both the new professionals and the incoming celebrities.

'The new dancers are the next generation of *Strictly*, just as the others were when they joined. The current pros are not just great dancers, they'll be there to guide the new pros too. *Strictly* is the best team to work with, so give it your best.

'To the new celebrities, my advice would be that this is not a sprint, this is a marathon, so pace yourself mentally, pace yourself physically. You need to open yourself to the show, because if you're not going to give your whole personality, all 100 per cent, people will sense that, and you want to win the hearts of the people. Also, work hard on the technique – it always pays off in the end.'

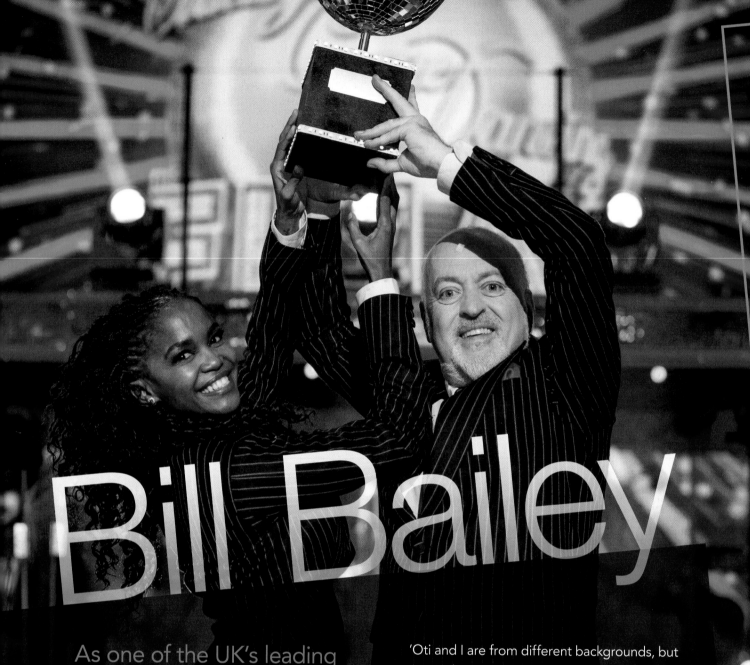

Bill Bailey

As one of the UK's leading comedians, Bill Bailey usually plays for laughs, but when he took on the *Strictly* challenge, he couldn't have taken it more seriously. In fact, his commitment was music to the ears of dance partner Oti Mabuse.

'Oti and I are from different backgrounds, but we're similar in many ways, because we both have a strong work ethic and share the drive and ambition to do the best we can and give 100 per cent,' he says.

'At the beginning Oti said, "I want you to do as well as you can. I want to get the most out of you and I want you to get the most out of the experience." That's why we hit it off so well. She didn't know how I would be as a pupil because we'd never met, but it became apparent very early on that I was up for the challenge.'

Bill's hard work paid off as he won the nation's heart with his *Doctor Dolittle*-inspired Quickstep, his foot-tapping Couple's Choice dance to 'Rapper's Delight' and an unforgettable showdance to 'The Show Must Go On', which clinched his place in the *Strictly* Hall of Fame. But lifting the glitterball still came as a surprise to the Somerset-born comic.

'It was an amazing feeling,' he says. 'I never expected to be in the Final so it was a bit of a turn-up. It was like a tremendous kind of outpouring of joy, relief and excitement. And it made all of those early starts and hours of training worthwhile!'

A keen cyclist who also works out at the gym, Bill threw himself into the physical challenge, training for eight hours every day with Oti.

'I was out of my comfort zone, learning a completely new skill, and nothing prepares you for how physically demanding it is at the start,' he says. 'But I soon realised that the mental challenge, the concentration required to pull off a dance live on television, is equal to the physical challenge, which I hadn't anticipated. I learned that sometimes you just have to put aside any fear of failure and fling yourself into the experience. And it's a wonderful experience.'

Although a novice dancer, Bill clicked quickly with the moves and recalls a special moment in week 2, as he rehearsed the now-legendary 'Talk to the Animals' routine.

'The Quickstep was one of my favourite dances because it was the first proper ballroom we did,' he explains. 'I remember this moment of whirling around a rehearsal room with Oti, in hold, catching a glimpse of myself in a mirror and being amazed that I was even capable of doing this but exhilarated by the experience. I've always been envious of others who can whirl around with great elegance and style at a function. Then I looked in the mirror, and I was actually doing it.

'In that dance there's a triple step, called a scatter chassé. Oti said, "There is a step we could do, where you do three steps instead of two," then she looked to me as if to say, "It's quite difficult. You don't have to do it." But I understood the concept through my musical training, I did the three steps and it was like a light bulb went off

in her head, as if she was thinking, "If you can do that, perhaps you could do all these other things." That opened up a door to possibilities. That's when I realised that I might be able to improve and learn more.'

The pair's memorable Couple's Choice dance to 'Rapper's Delight' by the Sugar Hill Gang was another favourite moment.

'When I was asked what song I'd be dancing to next week, I started to rap it and I immediately got a flurry of messages on my phone,' he recalls. 'One was from an old school friend who said, "I remember you rapping the entire ten-minute version at a party, when you were 18." It was a tricky, complex dance with lots of props, where you have to be in sync because you're not in hold as you are with the ballroom dances. You have to really concentrate, so pulling that off was a joyous experience and the whole Sugar Hill Gang sent me personal messages. While I loved every single dance for different reasons, that's the one which probably made the most impact.'

At 55, Bill is the oldest contestant to win the competition and he's hoping to be a trailblazer, encouraging many older men and women to take up dancing.

'There's definitely a reticence among older men to dance and they often feel a bit self-conscious,' he says. 'The term "dad dancing" is probably born out of the truth, because a lot of men feel uncomfortable on a dance floor, and the result is an embarrassed shuffle. But after seeing me do well in *Strictly*, I hope a lot of men and women will think, "It can be done and age is no barrier to learning a new skill." You might feel a little awkward at first, but if you immerse yourself in it and embrace it, it is liberating, and you can gain enormous confidence.'

Rhys
Stephenson

CBBC star Rhys Stephenson is stepping into the shoes of his co-star Karim Zeroual, who made the *Strictly* Final in 2019. But he first became a fan of the show thanks to 2015 winner Jay McGuiness.

'My dad turned on the TV just as Jay did his *Pulp Fiction* Jive and I remember thinking it was so cool,' he says. 'They started chilled, then the music switched tempo, they just exploded and my jaw hit the ground. After that, I needed to see him win and I became a huge fan.

'I love the idea of doing such a cool routine to great music. Sometimes I listen to music and think, "That would be a really good Paso Doble," and I can see it in my head! So it's always been a pipe dream, and seeing how much fun Karim had made me realise this show is as awesome as it seems.'

Born in South London, Rhys joined the National Youth Theatre at 13 and, while studying at Westminster University, he launched his career as a presenter on the student TV channel, winning a national broadcasting award. He joined CBBC in 2016 and has presented *Newsround*, *The Dengineers* and *Blue Peter*. After announcing his *Strictly* news, Rhys posted a video of his family's hilarious reaction with his two sisters screaming with excitement.

'Both my sisters are very excited about it,' he says. 'They'll all watch and my sisters will be doing their best to stay composed, but there might be a moment where they lose themselves and get too excited! My mum and dad will be very composed. They are a very supportive family and fiercely protective, which is wonderful, but they're also the first to point out if I do something wrong.'

That strong family background means Rhys is ready to face the judges and welcomes their critiques.

'The judges want you to do the best you can,' he explains. 'I look at it in the same way as when my parents disciplined me – they do it out of love, because they want me to be the best version of myself.'

An after-school street-dance class is the only formal experience the 27-year-old presenter has had on the floor, but he says it may help him with learning routines.

'I've got good rhythm – I've always enjoyed dancing and having fun with it. I've never done a dance in hold, so ballroom is completely new to me. But I trust myself, I trust my rhythm and I'll trust my partner, because that's where my strength is going to come from.'

Rhys has promised to bring the humour and energy that makes him a CBBC favourite and is most looking forward to the Jive. But he's keen to show a serious side too.

'The Jive is so dynamic, with all the kicks,' he says. 'I've got long legs so if I can use them correctly, that would be great. But I can't wait to do a serious dance like the Paso so I can scare people a bit and look intense. I'll be practising that face in the mirror and maybe doing Liam Neeson's famous *Taken* speech to get me in the mood!'

As a music lover, Rhys is also itching to get in front of Dave Arch's fabulous band in the studio.

'I'm looking forward to our first rehearsal with the band, because the live music is going to be electric,' he says. 'No matter how much you rehearse in the studio with a track, live music completely transforms your performance and your body does things you didn't even know you could. It unlocks something and it's amazing.'

Rhys says the best thing about *Strictly* so far has been the reaction from the public.

'It's been wonderful having people come up to me and be really excited,' he says. 'The ladies in my church are beside themselves and constantly asking about it. That kind of support has been really awesome.'

Nancy Xu

Returning for her third series, *Strictly* pro Nancy Xu is paired with children's presenter Rhys Stephenson and they're both bubbling over with enthusiasm.

'I am very excited to be partnering Rhys,' she says. 'I feel blessed. He's a lovely guy. Plus, he is so full of energy that the first time we met I said, "Oh my gosh, his energy with my energy might be too much for the camera."'

For the launch show, Nancy surprised her new partner at his CBBC studio in Manchester and the pair tried a couple of steps on the day. While Rhys still has a lot to learn, the talented teacher was instantly impressed with her new pupil.

'We tried a simple Jive kick, which he picked up very quickly,' she explains. 'I also tried him in a ballroom-hold position and his shape was good. For men, if you have never tried ballroom, the hold is really important, so I think he has huge potential in both Latin and ballroom, and he's a fast learner.'

A tough cookie, Nancy has told Rhys she will work him hard in training so he can get the maximum enjoyment out of the live show.

'I told Rhys that I want him to enjoy his journey and have fun,' she says. 'But obviously in the rehearsal room it is going to be tough, because on Saturday night I want him to relax and enjoy the dancing performance. I also told him I'm a very strict teacher and said, "Just watch my eyes in the rehearsal room, not my face," because sometimes when I'm serious and deeply focused, my face might look cross. But I also told him not to be scared – because I'm really lovely!'

Latin queen Nancy joined *Strictly* in 2019. Born in China, she has competed all over the world and has numerous titles to her name.

Now an established part of the *Strictly* team, Nancy says reuniting with her fellow dancers and meeting the four new pros in the group dances was a special moment.

'I feel really blessed that I am working with people who all have the same passion,' she says. 'We all have a deep love for what we do, and dancing together is just this amazing moment I look forward to every year.

'The four new dancers are really hard workers, very respectful and brilliant dancers. They all have lovely personalities and warm hearts. It doesn't feel like they are the new pros. They feel more like friends we've known for a long time. I love all of them.'

Dancing with her first celebrity partner, Nancy is excited for this season.

'I want to bring everything out in Rhys,' she says. 'I want to do my best for him because it's my responsibility – I'm in charge of the dance quality. I also want my partner to enjoy his journey on *Strictly*. Then we have a goal. We want to get in the Final and we want to get the glitterball! As a competitor, you always want to be there, so you have to aim high!'

The Elephant in the Ballroom

A trumpeting elephant, a crawling crocodile and several cows, sheep and chickens graced the *Strictly* dance floor in series 18, but animal-loving viewers have nothing to worry about.

They were all created with the magic of augmented reality (AR), a special effect that allows the studio to become a fantasy land. The technique, used in many of the dances last year, also saw Janette Manrara and HRVY encased in a snow globe, Clara Amfo dancing on a spinning record, cars and London buses racing across the floor and ice castles towering over the contestants.

The incredible effects are created by Potion Pictures, the designers already behind the graphics shown on the screens and projected onto the dance floor.

First, the images and designs are created using computer software. Ideas are usually finalised by Monday or Tuesday on a *Strictly* week, to ensure they have time to get the details right.

Next, infrared trackers, known as StarTrackers, are placed on top of the studio cameras and, during the live broadcast, they fire an infrared laser at reflective discs in the ceiling and around the set, which tell the software where the cameras are and how they are moving. The graphic can then be placed over the real scene being shot by the cameras and tracked in the same way, so that it looks like the graphic is part of the live scene.

Putting AR into a live dance show is not without its challenges, as Potion's Senior Designer Joe Phillips explains.

'Although my graphics look like they're being shot by the camera, they are actually over the lens and being fed in,' he explains. 'We can't have the dancers perform in front of it and we have to make sure they never move behind the image, but we can cheat perspective and make it look like they are walking under it, by moving the camera around.'

Because the graphics are over the lens, there's nothing visible in the studio, so the live audience, judges and contestants are not able to see the scenes the viewers enjoy at home. This means the dancers are effectively reacting to a blank space.

Before he comes up with his amazing designs, Joe liaises with the producers and choreographers as well as the dancers themselves.

'The dancers often have a lot of input,' he says. 'For example, Janette was very involved with the AR for the Street/Commercial [number] she danced with HRVY to "A Sky Full of Stars" by

Coldplay. They were watching the stars on the rooftop of a skyscraper and the buildings drop away so it has an amazing 3D effect. Janette had very specific areas where she wanted to have the AR work and it was all built into the dance. We are very happy to have guidance from choreographers and dancers, because they give us direction and understanding of how they will incorporate it into the dances, which works better than if we were just to have graphics added on top.'

One of the challenges with a live broadcast, especially on a show based around music and dance, is that the AR technology causes a tiny time lag.

'*Strictly* runs like clockwork, so to have this added technology on top was an extra challenge,' says Joe. 'By the time the video gets to us, has composites added and gets back to Series Director Nikki Parsons, it is delayed by a few frames, which means that the gallery has to run a delayed system alongside the normal working system. Everyone in the gallery has headphones on because the audio and the lighting are delayed by the AR technology, so they are switching between their normal working systems and the delayed working system. During the next video link they switch back, because there's a little bit of a jump, so Nikki has to be very clever about how to cut in and out of AR mode to make sure

no jump can be seen on TV screens. Nikki has such a big job to do, but she was brilliant, very understanding. We couldn't have done what we did without Nikki and Lighting Director Dave Bishop, who took it all in their stride.'

Augmented reality featured in an average of three dances a week in the last series, with amazing themes including a farm full of animals for Jamie Laing's Quickstep, the *Strictly Express* train for Caroline Quentin's American Smooth to '9 to 5 (Morning Train)' by Sheena Easton and the stunning ice castles in Maisie Smith's *Frozen II* routine.

'Towards the end of the series we got more ambitious because the producers had got used to how the technology works and we had more understanding of what works well and what viewers like, so we could see the full potential of what could be done,' says Joe.

'HRVY and Janette's Semi-final snow globe was one of my favourites, because it worked really well in the context of the dance, but it wouldn't have been easy for a set build to replicate a big glass ball.

'But I also loved the elephant at the end of Bill Bailey's Dr Dolittle dance, because it was funny – a nice humorous touch – and it made everyone happy.'

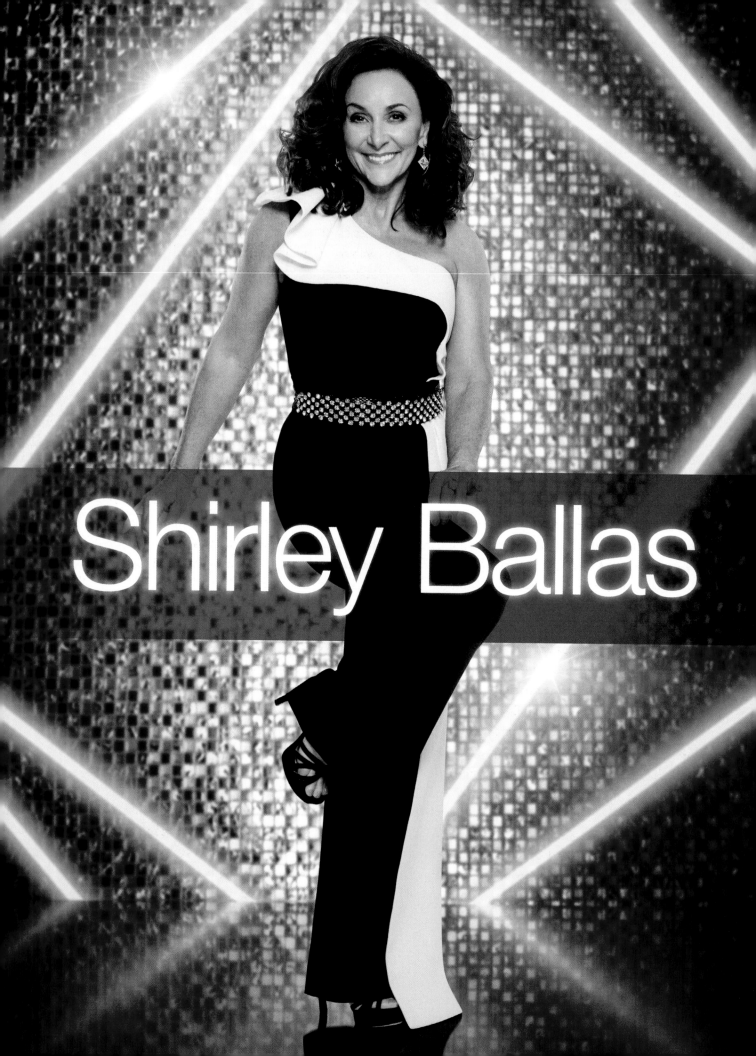

Head judge Shirley Ballas is thrilled to be returning for her fifth series and promises that the latest *Strictly* will take viewers 'to the moon and back'.

'This series will go at full pelt,' she says. 'Over the next 13 weeks we are going to have so much fun. I'm looking forward to Movie Week, Halloween and all the themed weeks, and we can't wait to bring some *Strictly* joy into the living rooms of the nation.'

Former Latin champ Shirley is impressed by the new *Strictly* stars and says the mix hits the perfect note for the new series.

'The whole cast looks super-competitive,' she says.

For Shirley, the mixture of sports personalities, presenters, chefs, actors and comedians has something for everyone – and she's convinced the class of 2021 will be an entertaining bunch.

'I climbed Kilimanjaro with Dan Walker, so I can't wait to see if his dancing is as good as his camping skills,' she says. 'I did a cooking show with AJ Odudu and she is a laugh a minute, pure fun. I'm looking forward to seeing if Tilly Ramsay's dancing compares to her cooking.

'I can't wait to see Judi Love doing a little shaking and baking, and *Dragons' Den* star Sara Davies is going to be great to watch. It's just a great line-up.'

The inclusion of Adam Peaty, fresh from bagging two gold medals at the Tokyo Olympics, is also a bonus.

'It's great to have Adam Peaty in an Olympic year,' says Shirley. 'He's trained all his life and now he's learning a totally new skill on an even footing with everybody else – that deserves a gold medal in itself!'

This year, Shirley, Craig and Motsi are welcoming a familiar face to the judges' desk, in the form of Anton Du Beke.

'I've known Anton for most of our competitive lives and he has always represented the show in such a tasteful, beautiful manner,' she says. 'Now he's got the opportunity to be on the panel, which I know is close to his heart, and I couldn't be more delighted.

'He has recently competed on the show, so he'll have great empathy and be sensitive to the way the couples feel when they're coming down the stairs, because last year that's where he was. And, of course, he'll bring Anton. Anton is a force to be reckoned with in himself!'

Shirley says last year's Final, which saw Bill Bailey sweep to victory, was a game-changer.

'I was delighted that Bill's talent and hard work was recognised by the public. He took no prisoners, and the fact that our winner was a man in his fifties made others think, "If he can do it, so can I." It's not just a young man's game. It depends how hard you work and what you're willing to put in.'

As the latest line-up take to the floor, the former Latin champ has some sound advice.

'First and foremost, work harder than you've ever worked before. Believe in yourself. Be 100 per cent focused on your professional as they will steer you in the right direction. But most of all, go out there, live every moment and enjoy the experience.'

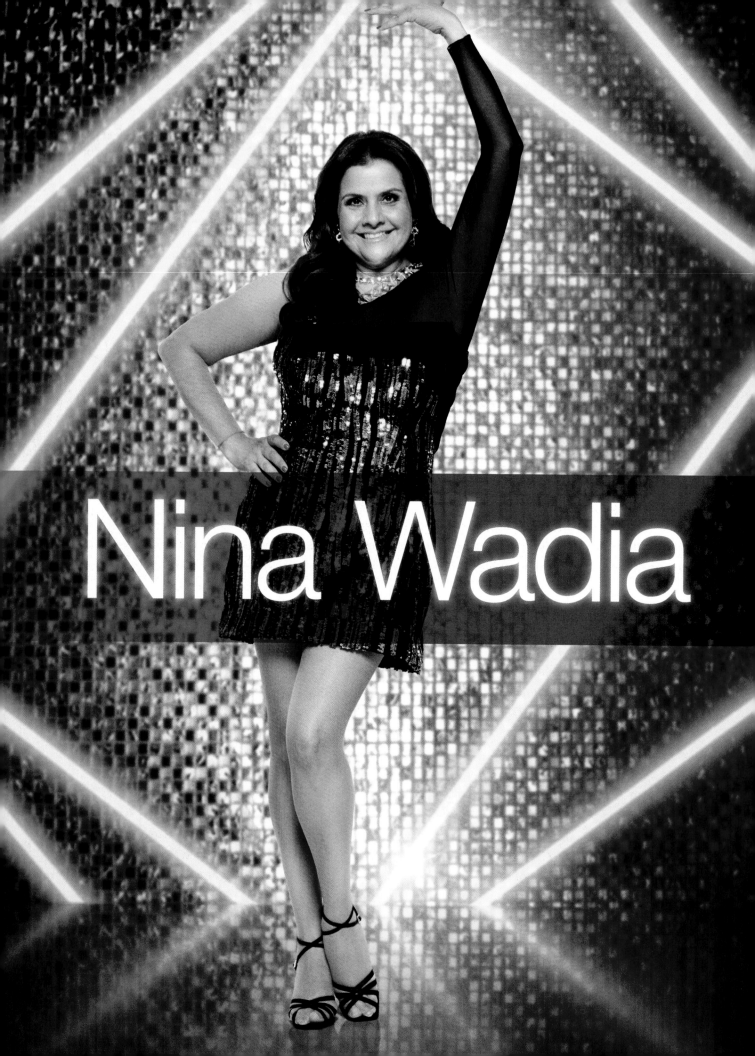

Nina Wadia

Comedian and actress Nina Wadia is hoping to bring a little humour to the dance floor in her routines – but that doesn't mean she's not taking the competition seriously.

'Like any job I do, I will put everything into it,' she says. 'I will take it seriously, but I need to have the comedy in order to get through. I can't take the glitz and glamour side seriously, but what I can take seriously is the technical side. I watched Jake Wood in *Strictly* and I thought he was brilliant because he threw himself into it, as did current champ Bill Bailey. I love people who just go for it, and it doesn't matter what they look like. That's what I'm going to do.'

The former *EastEnders* star predicts she will be drawn to the Latin style and might struggle with the upright hold positions of the sedate ballroom dances.

'I think the Argentine Tango is the sexiest dance I've ever seen,' she says. 'I'd love to learn how they flick their legs in all different directions. But I genuinely want to learn to do all of the dances. I want to know how the incredible pros get everyone who doesn't know the dances to the standard you see on the show, and I want to improve on what I can do.'

Born in Mumbai, Nina moved to Hong Kong at the age of nine and started her career writing comedy sketches while studying for her A levels. She sprang to fame as one of the four principals in the BBC sketch show *Goodness Gracious Me* and has since starred in *Still Open All Hours* and numerous films, including *Bend It Like Beckham* and the 2019 remake of *Aladdin*.

Although a novice in all things Latin and ballroom, Nina was a keen dance student as a child and loves a boogie.

'When I was very little, my mum sent me to Bharatanatyam classes, which is an Indian classical dance, and I did that until I was eight,' she says. 'In Hong Kong, I studied tap until I was about 17, but then everything stopped. But if you put any song on at a wedding, I'm the first on the dance floor and last off.'

While Nina could be a mover, the *Strictly* makeover is a complete change of style for her.

'I'm very much a T-shirt-and-jeans girl,' she says. 'I get dressed up for things when I have to, if I make TV appearances or if a character demands it. But when I played Zainab Masood in *EastEnders*, I told them to make her as plain as possible, because I don't like sitting in the make-up chair for too long.'

Even so, Nina, 52, is looking forward to the themed weeks.

'I'm really looking forward to Movie Week, and Halloween might be fun as well, because we can really become a character,' she says. 'Hair and make-up and wardrobe asked me if I was going to be in character for the dances and I said I would. They're amazing. No other make-up or hair team or wardrobe is ever going to compare to these guys.'

Nina, who is married to composer Raiomond Mirza and has two children, has had mixed reactions from the family.

'My daughter's very happy and my son said, "Don't embarrass me, Mum,"' she laughs.

The talented actress says her competitive side wants to get her to the Final, but her real mission is to entertain.

'Part of me wants to do the best I can do, but I want to have fun doing it,' she says. 'I want to make sure that, for the 90-second dance, people are entertained and having fun watching, and I want to enjoy every minute that I am given by the audience.'

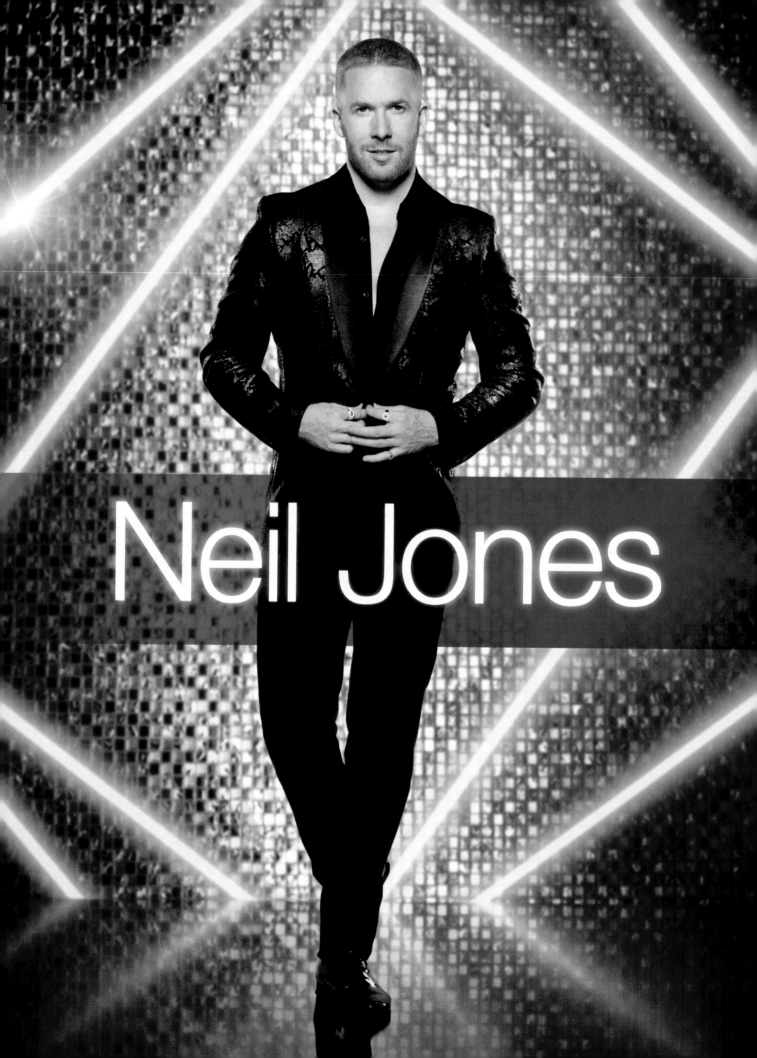

Neil Jones

When Neil Jones met his new dance partner, Nina Wadia, it was on a boat on the Thames with Windsor Castle towering behind – a scene befitting a queen of comedy.

'Someone else was driving the boat as we approached and Nina was trying to get a look at her mystery partner, but she could just see sunglasses and a shirt, so she thought it was Giovanni,' laughs Neil. 'We got on like a house on fire and were talking about all sorts of things straight away.'

Working with a comedian and actress, Neil plans to incorporate humour into their routines whenever appropriate.

'We're trying to find as many comedy elements as possible because *Strictly* is all about entertainment, and Nina is so funny,' he says. 'What we discovered when we were talking is that we're similar in outlook. We can be light-hearted, like to joke around and we both like comedy, but we also understand that it takes a lot of work to get comedy right. Being funny is not an easy thing, and you have to take it seriously in order for it to be funny. It's similar with dancing. You need to work hard to make it entertaining.'

Although it was not easy to try out the dance moves on a rocking boat, Neil got a brief glimpse of Nina's potential.

'We did a few kicks for a Jive and some spinning around, but because we were on a boat, I couldn't really see what she could do.

'I think Nina's strengths will be in the performance, because of her acting skills. I think finding the storyline for each dance will help her. She's going to be a great performer, so I'm hoping the moves are up there with that!'

In their first meeting, Neil put Nina's mind at rest, telling her he wouldn't be too hard a taskmaster.

'I said that we're going to enjoy it as much as possible,' he says. 'There are so many ways to do each thing and it's my job to find the best way to make it work with her.'

Born in a British army camp in Münster, Germany, Neil started dancing at three and trained in ballet, tap, modern, ballroom and Latin. He represented Finland, the Netherlands and the UK in his competitive career and holds 45 dance championship titles; to name a few, he is the eight-time British National, eight-time Dutch National, European and four-time World Latin Champion.

Neil joined *Strictly* in 2016 and, after Anton Du Beke's move to the judges panel, he jokes that he has now taken over the mantle of oldest male dancer.

'I now have to start wearing a shirt and tie to rehearsal and come in with my cup of tea, like Anton always did,' he laughs. 'But Anton will be a great judge. He's been in our position, so he knows exactly what we're going through, how hard everybody's working and what we need to do to help our celebrity improve.'

As well as the great couples' dances, Neil has revealed a sneak preview of the group numbers and says viewers are in for a treat.

'The group dances are really spectacular and they all feel like mini-movies,' he says. 'We've got an incredible opening number, a brilliant cowboy number and another dance where each of us is a famous character, and everyone's going to have fun trying to work out who is who. The choreography and the dancing are incredible. Every year we ask how we can improve on this and every year they manage to do it.'

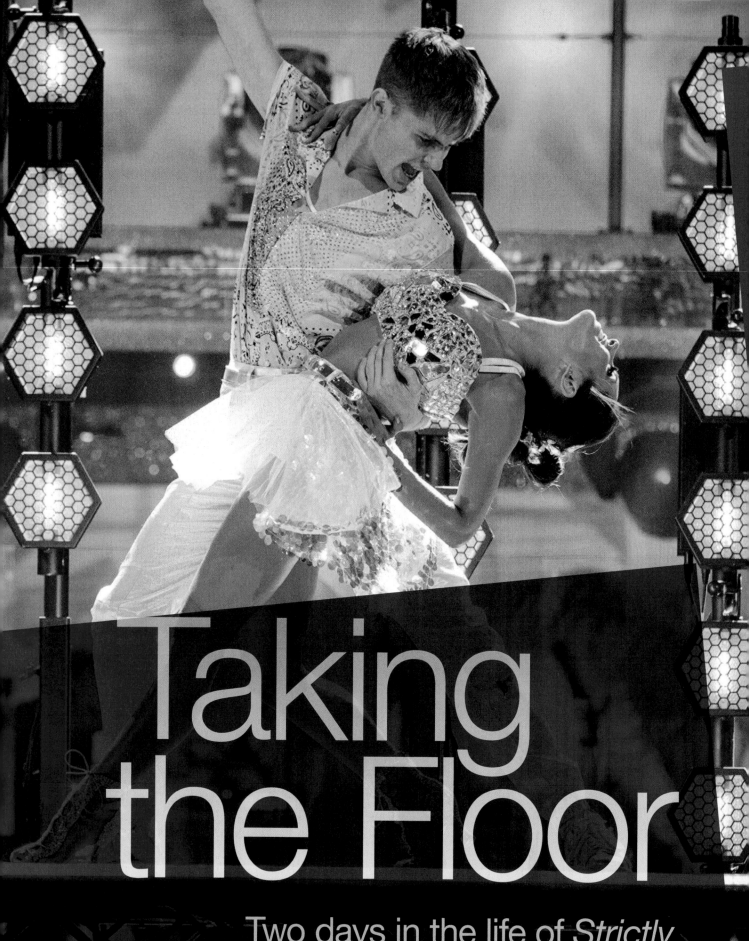

Taking the Floor

Two days in the life of *Strictly*
Floor Manager Alan Conley

Running a live show on prime-time TV requires forward planning, synchronisation and a lot of teamwork.

While Executive Producer Sarah James and Series Director Nikki Parsons oversee the show from the gallery, Floor Manager Alan Conley is the man on the ground, making sure it all runs smoothly in the studio.

'I'm Nikki's eyes and ears on the floor,' explains Alan, who has worked on the show for 14 years. 'She has a plan of what she wants throughout the day, and it's up to me to make sure everything happens at the right time, in the right place, and to convey her vision onto the studio floor. I make sure cameras, sound and lighting crews are all communicating with each other and relevant information is getting passed on.'

Alan's *Strictly* week begins on Friday, when the dancers rehearse in the studio for the first time, and then it's all systems go.

Here, he talks us through two days in his hectic *Strictly* life.

FRIDAY

On the Friday rehearsal, each couple comes onto the floor and has a strict 20 minutes each to rehearse their routine, which they run through three times to a music track, as the live band is not there. At the beginning of the series, when we have 15 couples, that takes over five hours.

After that, we block through the lighting positions – meaning we make sure all the dancers and the celebrities know where to stand for the opening of the show and the results and so on, for the purposes of lighting.

If you look closely at the studio floor, it is covered in little tape marks that I put down, which indicate where people stand. So, for example, when a couple is chatting with the judges, Tess stands on the yellow T and the contestants stand on a little blue T next to her. When the couples come down the stairs at the start of the show, there are numbers all over the floor, 1 to 15, indicating where each couple stands. They're spaced so that the camera can see all of them and each spot has its own spotlight. If they drift off left or right, they will be in darkness, so it's important they know where to stand at all times.

Throughout the rehearsal, I'm talking to Nikki in the gallery and passing on any changes she wants. It could be a costume alteration, or a prop that's in the wrong place, for example, and I pass that on to the relevant departments. But it works both ways; sometimes the dancers want to change things, which I will relate back to Sarah and Nikki, so I liaise between the talent and production.

Later in the day we usually rehearse our fabulous group dances, and towards the end of the day Tess and Claudia come into the studio to read through their links, and we look at their positions. This takes about 90 minutes, and I make sure they're happy with everything, and talk to them about any script changes needed.

Friday is also an important day for the props team, who need to make sure they can get each set on the floor and built in time. With the live show you've only got a minute during the video clips to set the giant props for our dancers and we need to make sure there is enough time. In some of our routines the dancers are flying in with

harnesses and this needs to be well rehearsed, as a lot of the time our celebrities have never done anything like this before.

A recent addition to our *Strictly* routines is augmented reality, where we can now project the impossible onto the dance floor, like having an elephant walking through the studio. This also takes time to look at on a Friday, so as you can see, it's a busy day.

SATURDAY

9 a.m.

Show day starts with the band call, which is probably my favourite part of the day, because there is no other show on TV that has a live orchestra like that and I get to listen to them playing the whole morning. The couples get to dance to the live track for the first time as well, and we look at the pyrotechnics and make sure they're all safe, and the dancers know where the fireworks will go off or when smoke will come across the floor. Then we rehearse the group dance before breaking for lunch at one.

2 p.m.

The dress rehearsal, where we run the show all the way through with everybody in costume, make-up and hair for the first time and with special effects, props and augmented reality.

This is a really important part of the day for me, because I have to make sure the dress rehearsal runs to time and everything's in the right place. Backstage is a military operation, with hair and make-up and wardrobe working flat out, and I have three Assistant Floor Managers (AFMs) who are running around throughout the day, making sure those departments have plenty of time to get everybody through – especially on themed weeks like Halloween. Last year, they wore fitness trackers and they clocked up 13 miles – so they basically did a half-marathon over the day. But they have worked with me for ten years, so it is a well-oiled machine.

Elstree's so big, it feels like the dancers go off and hide all over the place, but I know where they are because we've worked together for so long. But when we're in Blackpool, which has a huge backstage maze, they scatter all over the place and tracking them down is much harder. I would have to say Giovanni and Aljaž are probably the naughtiest – you have to keep them on a tight rein – but I love all the dancers and we have great fun together.

The early shows are the busiest for me, because there is a routine to *Strictly* with hair and make-up, wardrobe, rehearsals and band calls, and what time the celebrities come in. We try to keep it similar each week, so that they get used to the timings, but in the early weeks I'm still teaching the celebrities where they need to be, and with 15 couples the schedule is tight.

4.15 p.m.

The guest act comes in and has about 45 minutes to rehearse, along with our professional dancers. During this, I liaise with the record label and artist about the look of the performance, and discuss any special effects we have.

5 p.m.

The audience start coming into the auditorium and at 6 p.m., once they are all seated, our brilliant warm-up man, Stuart Holdham, entertains them and talks them through what will happen throughout the evening. Then, before the live show starts, we may pre-record the guest number or a group opening number.

7 p.m.

All set for the main show. The famous music starts and, after 14 years, I still get a great buzz. With a live show, you only get one chance to get it right, so there's a lot more pressure than a pre-recorded show, but that just adds to the excitement of Saturday night.

In terms of props, staging and special effects, the show has changed over the years. When I started, the biggest prop was probably Anton's cane and hat, but now we have all sorts – boats and sleighs going across the floor, a lighthouse, augmented reality and fireworks. It's much busier, but it has taken the show to another level.

Alan and Brian Conley on Series 15

Of course, I have loved every series, but series 15 is especially memorable for me because my brother, Brian Conley, was one of the contestants. He had a brilliant partner in Amy and everyone on set loved working with him, but it was strange having to boss my older brother about and tell him where to stand. But I did enjoy watching him dance.

My favourite week is Musicals Week, because I love musicals and all the big props that we have – like a *Chitty Chitty Bang Bang* car – are fantastic. The wardrobe, hair and make-up team do a fantastic job and I love listening to the band playing songs from the musicals.

Throughout the year, I work on many TV shows, but *Strictly* is certainly one of my favourite jobs. I love the idea, the costumes, the way it's lit. The live music and having the band on the floor makes it so special. More than anything, every year is different – and more magical than the last.

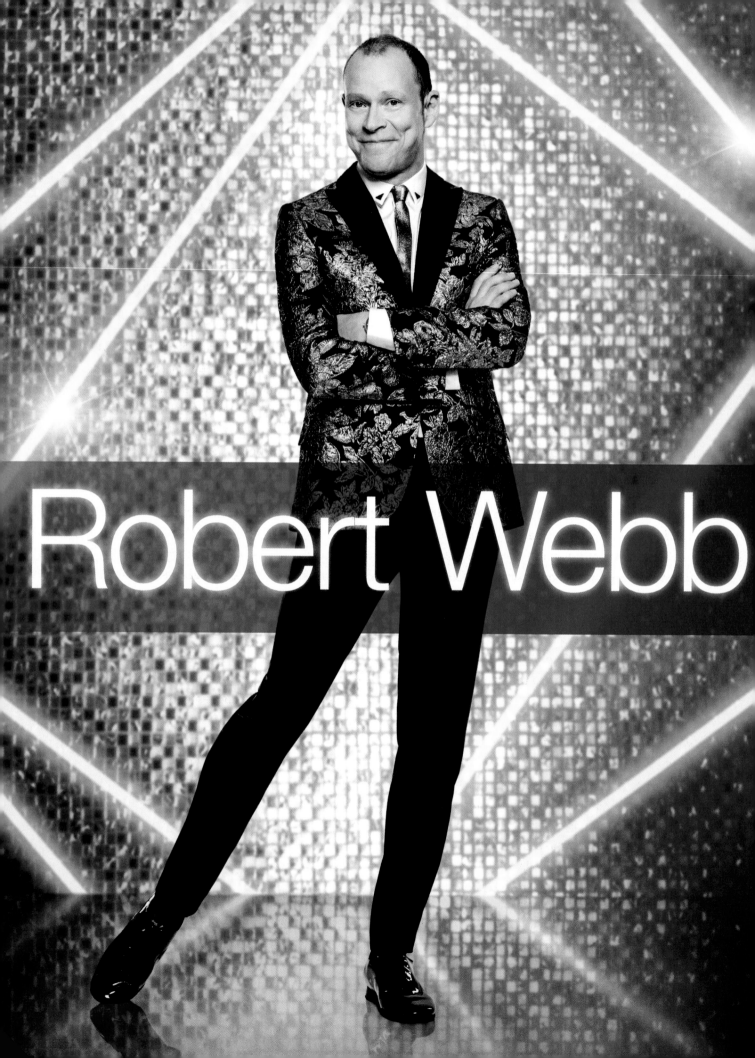

Robert Webb

Actor and author Robert Webb is a long-standing fan of the show but says a recent health scare prompted his decision to take the *Strictly* challenge.

'Almost two years ago I had open-heart surgery for a mitral valve prolapse,' he explains. 'Since then, my attitude has been that this is no time to be cool and sit at the edges watching other people do the dancing. If you've got something to offer, it's time to offer it. Also, I've spent the last few years writing and I felt the need to reconnect with the audience as a performer. Plus, *Strictly* looks like a lot of fun. Hard, but fun.'

Lincolnshire-born Robert met comedy partner David Mitchell at Cambridge University, where they were both members of the Footlights. They went on to forge a long and successful TV career, starring in *Peep Show* and the Bafta-winning series *That Mitchell and Webb Look*.

In 2009, Robert performed the iconic *Flashdance* routine, for *Let's Dance for Comic Relief*. Despite winning the competition, he thinks there is room for improvement.

'The live first heat was the first time I got through the dance from start to finish without stopping and looking at the choreographer, not knowing what to do next,' he says. 'I was in all kinds of terror before that screen went up, but hopefully I won't be like that on *Strictly*. We get a bit longer to rehearse the routines, so I won't be so badly prepared, and also I have a partner, so it won't be quite as nerve-racking.'

The routine, which had Robert in a wig and sleeveless leotard, also prepared him for the Lycra and sparkles coming his way this autumn.

'I've shown I'm not afraid of an extreme costume and showing a bit of flesh,' he says. '*Strictly* is a much more sedate affair, but if it's not going to upset anyone, I'm up for more or less anything – within the laws of public decency!'

Although Robert is guaranteed to keep viewers laughing, away from the floor he is deadly serious when it comes to the dances and the contest.

'The part of the audience that recognises me from *Peep Show* or *That Mitchell and Webb Look* might think that I'm here to send it up, but I'm absolutely not,' he says. 'I'll be doing it as straight as I can. I want to make a romantic dance very romantic and make the passionate dances, like the Paso Doble, very solemn and a little scary. I'm anxious to reassure the judges, as well as the audience, that I'm not here to muck around.'

As a newcomer to Latin and ballroom, Robert isn't sure which dance will suit him best but says he is most looking forward to the Paso Doble. When it comes to the themed weeks, he is hoping to make it to Halloween – for a special reason.

'Halloween will be the second anniversary of my heart surgery,' he reveals. 'So maybe that will be the show where I get my scar out – covered in glitter.'

Looking at the competition, Robert thinks everyone is in with a chance of taking the glitterball, and says he just wants to stay as long as he can.

'It would be lovely to win, but in the first couple of weeks I'll just be hanging on for dear life, and if the judges give me a score of more than one I'll be happy,' he jokes. 'But if I get halfway through, I expect I'll become very competitive and start poisoning other people's energy drinks and setting trip wires for Greg Wise!'

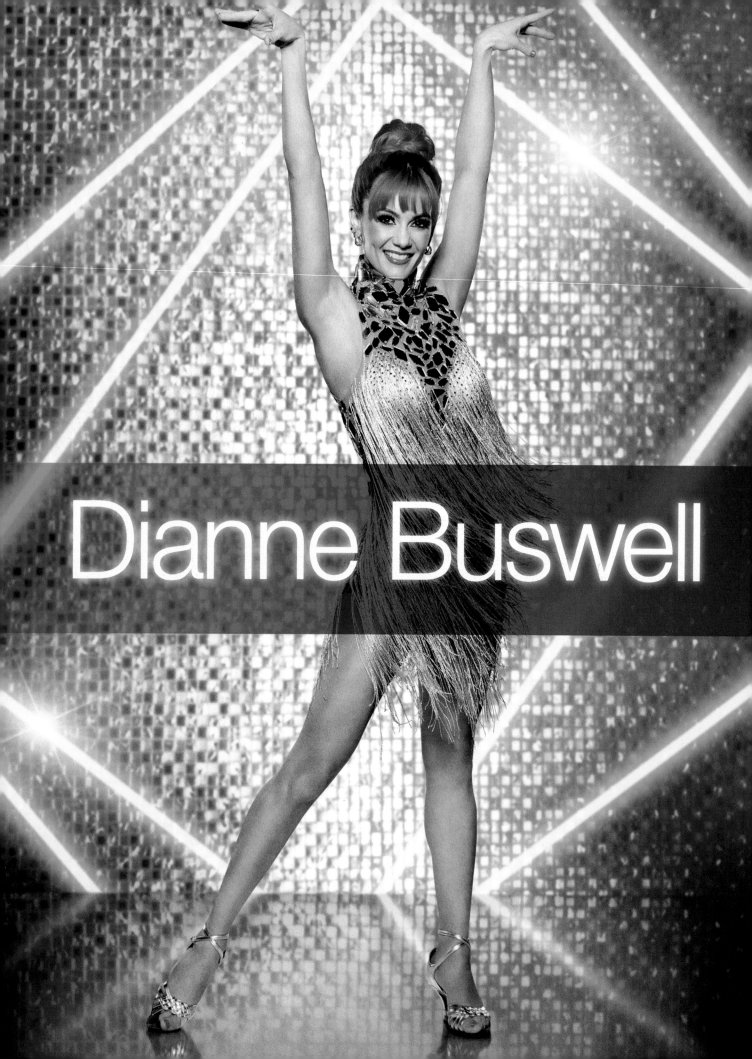

Dianne Buswell

Partnered with actor Robert Webb this season, Dianne Buswell is planning to combine a huge dose of fun with some serious dancing.

'Robert is naturally funny, but he really wants to take this competition very seriously,' she says. 'He is in it to learn to dance, so there will be humour in some of the routines, but with good dancing as well. Viewers will be laughing with him, not at him.

'Personality wise, he's everything I could want in a partner. He's absolutely hilarious and he makes me laugh so much, but he wants to take this seriously. In the first few steps I taught him, I can see so much potential. He's got a lot of character and charisma and he's really prepared to put in the hard work, which is very exciting.'

Like much of the nation, Dianne has watched Robert's iconic *Flashdance* routine for *Let's Dance for Comic Relief* and says there are some promising moves amid the comedy.

'I have watched it many times and it's brilliant, that's why I'm so excited,' she says. 'The potential is definitely in there.'

The Australian pro believes Robert's long career as an actor and comedian will help in the performance.

'He can play a character, which I think will be one of his big scoring cards,' she says. 'Each dance has a character and each dance has a storyline, which he will portray very well.'

Born in Bunbury, Western Australia, Dianne partnered brother Andrew as a young dancer. She became Australian Open Champion and four-time Amateur Australian Open finalist, before joining the Australian version of *Strictly*, *Dancing with the Stars*. She moved to the UK series in 2017, and the following year she reached the Final with social-media star Joe Sugg. In series 18, she partnered The Wanted singer Max George.

'Max was really fun, the loveliest guy,' she says. 'He is quite shy and wasn't very confident about dancing in front of millions of people, which is fair enough, so I had to bring him out and reassure him that he could do it. And every week he did. We had a great time.'

This year, Dianne is hoping she'll have more time to get creative and throw a few surprises into her dance routines.

'I'm looking forward to bringing out a really fun and interesting side to my choreography this year,' she says.

'I want to work hard and make Robert feel comfortable every Saturday on the dance floor. I want him to have the best experience possible.'

Dianne is also thrilled to be reunited with her fellow dancers for the group dances.

'Throughout the weeks that we were rehearsing, it felt so good to be back together, and being in a room with all those fabulous dancers is quite something else. It's crazy being with people who share such passion and work so hard. I absolutely loved every second of it.'

Ballroom Blitz

The musical arrangements performed by Dave Arch, the orchestra and the *Strictly* singers aren't the only numbers to come out of the show. From the judges' scores to the dimensions of the dance floor, stats and figures are all part of the series, so here's your guide to *Strictly* in numbers.

THE WINNING PROFESSIONS

From politicians to presenters, bloggers to Olympic gold medallists, contestants from all walks of life have tried out their fancy footwork on the floor. But here are the professions that have bagged the most glitterballs in the main series:

* **Presenters:** 5
* **Soap stars:** 3
* **Sports personalities:** 3
* **Musicians/singers:** 3
* **Actors (non-soap):** 2
* **Comedians:** 1
* **Models:** 1
* **Politicians:** 0

THE PERFECT 10

Over 18 series a total of 893 perfect 10s have been awarded, with the most going to the classic ballroom dances. The scores on the doors are as follows:

* **Ballroom:** 275
* **Latin:** 196

FULL MARKS

So far, 67 dances have been awarded the perfect score in the main series, with Jill Halfpenny's series 2 Jive being the first to achieve the highest honour.

In series 18, six top scores were awarded, with HRVY and Janette Manrara's Street/Commercial routine in week 6 the first to sweep the board – making it the earliest perfect score in any series to date.

Christmas specials have seen the judges embrace the season of goodwill, awarding a total of 14 perfect scores over the years.

DRESSED TO DANCE

An average *Strictly* series requires over 1,000 outfits, all designed by costume queen Vicky Gill. An average of 3.5 million rhinestones will be glued onto the costumes throughout the series.

RECORD BREAKERS

Giovanni Pernice holds the record for the current professional with the most 10s awarded, totalling 68. Oti is the current female professional with the most 10s to her name, having been awarded 60. The pair also share the record for perfect scores, with seven each.

GLOBETROTTING

Strictly is one of the world's most successful TV formats. The show has been licensed to 60 countries and in 2020 Mongolia was the most recent country to license this hit entertainment format. In the US the show is known as *Dancing with the Stars* and in Germany as *Let's Dance*. Both countries have also aired a kids' version of the show.

BUILDING THE DANCE DREAM

* The *Strictly Come Dancing* set is built on the George Lucas Stage at Elstree Studios in Hertfordshire.
* It is transported by 14 trucks, each 40 feet long – about the same-sized fleet as a large rock-and-roll tour.
* The set consists of around 2,000 sections of scenery, with 7,000 bolts to hold all the elements together.
* It takes approximately 160 person days to build, with a crew of 10 working for 16 days.
* The expertly sprung dance floor measures 10 metres × 16 metres.
* Claudia's area is approximately 9 metres in diameter.
* There are around 4,000 metres of LED ribbon lighting.

Craig Revel Horwood

Strictly judge Craig Revel Horwood is not always easy to please and is never afraid to speak his mind – but he's thrilled with the new line-up of *Strictly* stars.

'The group is terrific, all great personalities,' he says. 'And they're completely different – from elite sports personalities to a *Dragons' Den* businesswoman and a comedian.'

With 18 series under his belt, Craig has seen hundreds of hopeful celebrities take to the dance floor for the first time and has been casting an experienced eye over the latest cohort of contestants.

'I recently met AJ Odudu, who is absolutely adorable, and she was with her mum, who is a *Strictly* superfan,' he says.

'Sara Davies is fabulous. I adore watching her on *Dragons' Den*. She is going to be a joy in the show. Dan Walker is very tall, which means he could look great in the ballroom dances.

'I've seen Judi Love on *Loose Women* and she seems like a lot of laughs, with a really positive attitude. Rhys Stephenson is young and spirited so I'll enjoy seeing how he gets on with the Latin dances.'

As the first ever deaf contestant, *EastEnders* star Rose Ayling-Ellis has a challenge ahead, but Craig believes she is more than up for it. 'Rose is one of the most exciting bookings,' he says. 'I think she's going to amaze everyone.'

Craig has high hopes for the other actors among the new cast, whose day job helps them get into character and also teaches them some movement.

'Katie McGlynn will be elegant and look fantastic on the floor, but whether she's got rhythm or not remains to be seen,' says Craig. 'I've met Nina Wadia and she's fun, with a lovely outlook on life.

'We've all seen Robert Webb dancing in his brilliant *Flashdance* routine for *Comic Relief*, so we know he has fantastic movement and rhythm, but can he do something more technical? I'm reserving judgement on Greg Wise, because I haven't seen him move.'

As a musician, McFly guitarist Tom Fletcher certainly has rhythm.

'Artists from boybands have been fantastic so far,' says Craig. 'So that's a lot of expectation to live up to!'

The new line-up also boasts a chef and a baker, who will be cooking up a storm on the dance floor.

'*Bake Off* winner John Whaite is fantastic in the kitchen, but can he actually bring that to the dance floor? Being part of the first male same-sex couple is going to be interesting to see. Tilly Ramsay is composed and together and she'll put her heart and soul into it.'

For the sports personalities, Craig says, 'Rugby players have done well in the past, so I hope I can say the same for Ugo Monye.

'Finally, Adam Peaty won two gold medals at the Tokyo Olympics and is literally straight off the plane and into *Strictly*.'

As well as a new line-up of stars, Craig is looking forward to welcoming pro dancer Anton Du Beke to the judging panel.

'Anton has been great when he's filled in during previous shows, so I'm so pleased for him,' he says. 'He can give us the inside information on what it's actually like to walk down those stairs and dance in front of 12 million people, which is not easy. Anton will be a really great addition to our judging family.'

Sara Davies

Dragons' Den star Sara Davies is going from boardroom to ballroom, and she couldn't be more excited.

'I feel like I've waited my whole life, hoping that one day I might get asked to do *Strictly*,' she says. 'When I got that call, I tried to play it cool, saying, "Yes, that's something we could talk about." In reality, I was thinking, "Yes! Sign me up now!"'

Although she has no dance experience herself, Sara is not the first member of her family to take to the floor.

'My dad, who's now 70, did amateur dancing from the age of 10 to 16,' she reveals. 'I asked him why and he said he thought it would be a great way to pick up girls, so he joined dance classes and absolutely loved it. He's even danced at Blackpool.

'Ever since *Strictly* started, we have got together as a family on a Saturday night and we all crowd round the TV to watch it. My mum, my sister and I are enamoured by the costumes, the hair, the make-up and the razzmatazz, but my dad says, "Shh, I'm watching the steps." He's really into the specifics of the dancing.'

After signing up for the show, Sara says her parents were 'in shock'.

'They're both really excited, but Dad was worried that I wanted to do it for him, to make him proud. He told me, "Don't feel under any pressure, pet. Just enjoy the process. It's not the end of the world if you don't go that far." Clearly, he's not optimistic about the dance skills he's seen in me for the last 37 years!'

Sara's two sons, Oliver, seven, and four-year-old Charlie, are taking her new adventure in their stride.

'All their friends at school are saying, "I can't believe your mum's on *Strictly*," and I've showed them a bit of the show, but I don't think they get it,' she says. 'After watching me on *Dragons' Den* they said, "Mummy, that's rubbish. You don't look like a dragon and that's not a proper den!" So I can't wait to see what they make of *Strictly*.'

Born in County Durham, Sara was running a successful company before she had even graduated with her business degree from the University of York. Her company now exports to 40 countries worldwide. In 2019, Sara became an investor on *Dragons' Den* and says she has been chatting to fellow Dragon and former *Strictly* star Deborah Meaden ahead of her own turn on the show.

'We have spent many a morning together and I ask her all about it,' she says. 'Deborah says it was the best experience of her life. She loved the dancing, the community, the atmosphere, and she told me if I ever got the chance, I should embrace it with both arms.'

Although she is excited about all the dances, Sara predicts she'll be 'more of a ballroom girl' than a Latin lover.

'I'm slightly nervous about the Samba and the really fast Latin ones and I think I will definitely be better at the ballroom dances with the slower pace – although I've been watching the Viennese Waltz and there's nothing slow about that one! Also, I'm nervous about wearing heels and jiggling about a lot. I am the sort of person who could absolutely go head over feet on the dance floor.'

Even so, Sara is looking forward to being glammed up with a *Strictly* makeover – and her mum can't wait either.

'My first day at the studio, my mum was texting me all day, saying, "Have you seen the dress yet?"' she says. 'I was so excited to meet the hair and the make-up team and the wardrobe team. Getting to work with the best teams in the world and have them make you look amazing is such a privilege. I'm living the dream.'

Aljaž Škorjanec

In past series he's danced with models, actresses and even a viscountess, but this year Aljaž Škorjanec is dancing with a Dragon.

The former *Strictly* champ was teamed with Durham businesswoman and *Dragons' Den* star Sara Davies under the Angel of the North, and says Northerners have been his lucky charm so far.

'It's the first time I've been up close to the Angel of the North and it was a beautiful sight,' he says. 'Sara is from up North, and I have had an amazing time on the show with Abbey Clancy, from Liverpool, and Gemma Atkinson, from Manchester. With one I won the show and the other I made the Final, but more importantly we got along brilliantly and so far it has been just like that with Sara. I'm really chuffed and very excited.'

Although he's yet to see the queen of the boardroom dance, Aljaž says her success in business proves she has an impressive focus, which will be useful in training.

'Sara is extremely eager to learn and keen to practise, which is exactly what any teacher wants to hear,' he says. 'It doesn't matter what your dancing experience is, as long as you throw yourself into it 100 per cent. I'm happy and she's going to be happy.

'She's an extremely successful woman, extremely driven, and just from meeting her for the first time, I get the impression that there is nothing that Sara Davies can't take on in her life!'

Sara's can-do attitude and warm personality have also impressed her new teacher, and he's hoping to put that across in the routines.

'Sara has a wonderful, positive personality,' he says. 'As far as I'm concerned, *Strictly* is about her, it's about our celebrities, and therefore I'm going to do everything I can to make her look amazing on the dance floor.

'In our first meeting I told her we were going to work hard, train as much as we possibly can, and I promised I would give her 150 per cent. Everything I do, everything I choreograph, every song I pick is for her and she just needs to trust me. The last thing I said was, "I promise we are going to have fun, every single step of the way."'

Brought up in a small town in Slovenia, Aljaž started dancing at five and became 19-time Slovenian Champion in ballroom, Latin and Ten Dance. He joined *Strictly* in 2013, bagging the glitterball with model and TV presenter Abbey Clancy. Since then, his partners have included Alison Hammond, Helen George, Daisy Lowe and Viscountess Emma Weymouth. Last year, he competed with DJ Clara Amfo and pulled off a near-perfect score for their week 4 Charleston.

'Clara was a joy to be around and a joy to dance with,' he says. 'She was such a huge fan of *Strictly* so every time she stepped on that floor she was living her dream, which was a beautiful thing to be a part of. I was so happy to be the plus one for Clara and I am never going to forget that Charleston, for the rest of my life.'

With Anton Du Beke on the judging panel rather than the dance floor this year, ballroom fan Aljaž will be the longest-serving male dancer competing, but he says no one could step into Anton's dancing shoes.

'Anton is the king of the ballroom, the king of *Strictly*,' he says. 'I'm never going to fill those shoes. I just hope I can carry his flag for a little while and I'm going to do my absolute best to make him proud as a judge, and his constructive criticism is always appreciated.'

At the start of the new series, Aljaž is bursting with enthusiasm.

'I can't wait to start dancing with Sara Davies on that floor,' he says. 'I'm looking forward to the first number, I'm looking forward to every single week, every single day in rehearsals. I'm going to cherish every moment. I'm so excited for this season – probably more than ever.'

Food for Fitness

Being a *Strictly* pro requires a high level of fitness and a LOT of energy. Whether they are rehearsing all day with a celebrity partner, touring or working out on their days off, the dancers' daily diet means eating well and choosing the right foods to fuel those hours on the go. Here, four of the show's pro dancers share their typical daily menus, and the recipe for a favourite treat.

GRAZIANO DI PRIMA

'My training is a combination of dance practice and gym sessions,' says Graziano. 'When I'm not on *Strictly* I usually train for two to three hours per day, but when I have a show I need to rehearse at least eight hours per day, so my schedule depends on how much I need to perform.'

Breakfast: A long coffee or cappuccino with a banana and sometimes Nutella. Or an English breakfast with scrambled eggs, mushrooms and bread. And coffee.

Lunch: Pasta, rice or tortellini with fresh tomato sauce, pesto or spaghetti carbonara. If I have to dance after lunch, I prefer plain pasta with olive oil and Parmesan cheese.

Snack: Greek yoghurt with granola and honey or some fruit. If I'm not at home, I'll take an energy bar. And, of course, a coffee.

Dinner: Meat or vegetable proteins, preferably chicken with vegetables or halloumi with potatoes or peas. My favourite dinner is homemade pizza.

NANCY XU

'When *Strictly* is not on, I do Pilates for an hour every morning,' says Nancy. 'Then I do cardio or dance practice after lunch, normally from 2 p.m. to 3 p.m. Sunday is a day off!'

Breakfast: Yoghurt with fruit (strawberries or bananas) and coffee, or two slices of homemade (by me) bread with smoked salmon and my homemade chilli sauce.

Lunch: I normally make a vegetable salad with Chinese cabbage, lettuce, broccoli and cauliflower, steamed, boiled or fried and dressed with a sauce. Recently I like to make fresh juice (strawberry, mango, kiwi fruit and water). I might also have a piece of 75 per cent dark chocolate and some crisps or nuts.

Dinner: For me, dinner is always important. Sometimes I will cook a typical Chinese dinner, such as white rice and Sichuan mapo tofu or white rice with cold aubergines. I might make vegetable soup or tomato and eggs with noodles. But I also like to make Italian dinners such as homemade seafood pasta or homemade pizza.

NADIYA BYCHKOVA

'On *Strictly* rehearsal days, we are dancing from 9 a.m. to around 6 p.m., so we burn plenty of energy,' says Nadiya. 'When I am not on *Strictly*,

I will do a home workout, go for a long, long walk or just walk on a treadmill at home, but most days I do some sort of activity.'

Breakfast: Porridge. If it's a rehearsal day I will make my coffee to go because I don't like to have my coffee in a rush, so I take it with me to work.

Lunch: Salad with chicken. I like something light at lunch so that I can carry on dancing and don't fall asleep!

Snacks: I like fruit in the morning, so maybe an apple or an orange. I also take rice cakes with me to snack on through the afternoon and keep the energy levels up.

Dinner: It depends how much time I have or how tired I am, and how much I have to cook, but I avoid junk food. So it could be some rice and chicken and some salad or maybe pasta. It's usually something Italian or Mediterranean. If I really want to treat myself I will have an indulgent dessert. I love to make tiramisu, but chocolate soufflé, served with vanilla ice cream, is my favourite. The family loves it when I make that.

JOHANNES RADEBE

'Good nutrition and regular exercise help improve my mood every day more than anything,' says Johannes. 'Home workouts have become a thing for me these past couple of months. I took up yoga online and I'm loving it.'

Breakfast: I swear by porridge.

Lunch: Panini sandwich, packing in carbohydrates. Cold meats with fresh bread.

Snacks: Fruits and nuts.

Dinner: Depends on the mood, but my favourite is a beef burrito.

Greg Wise

After 30 years of treading the boards, actor Greg Wise is keen to try a twirl on the dance floor – and he's hoping to follow in the footsteps of his close friend, current champ Bill Bailey.

'I've been around the block a few times and have never dreamt of trying to do something like this, so it's great to take on a challenge,' he says. 'It's all about living out of your comfort zone. I'm the oldest contestant this year and I've got to try and emulate Mr Bailey, because we're the same age.'

But the 55-year-old actor also has a deeply touching reason for joining the show – to pay tribute to his late sister, Clare.

'The night we do our first routine will be exactly five years since my sister died and she was a real disco diva,' he says. 'She was the dancer in the family, and she left this world in a glitterball coffin. As this show is all glittery and diva-ish and disco, I thought, "I have to do it for Clare."'

Born in Newcastle, Greg decided to study drama after falling in love with acting. He met wife Emma Thompson while starring in *Sense and Sensibility* in 1995, and she was behind his decision to do *Strictly*.

'I was going to say no, but Emma said, "You're mad, you've got to do it!"' he says. 'She's been filming solidly since January, making three films back to back, and we'd planned a really nice autumn and our first holiday in seven years. Over the space of that five-minute conversation, the entire autumn was kicked into the long grass, and here I am. But Emma's thrilled because she'll be able to relax and support me and watch every Saturday night – or as many Saturday nights as I survive.'

Greg also took advice from series-18 winner Bill before signing up.

'Bill said, "Well, it's a lot of work, but it's top japes," and I'm always on the lookout for top japes,' laughs Greg. 'He also told me you've got to look after your feet – to get my patent-leather ballroom shoes early and wear them around the house to break them in, so he was very helpful.'

Despite attending many a ball in period dramas, Greg has never learned ballroom dancing for a role.

'Ten years ago, I made *Walking on Sunshine*, which was a musical full of fabulous hits of the Eighties, and I danced a bit of Tango for a few seconds, but no more than that,' he says. 'If I've been required to dance for period films, it's always been a sort of Austenian line dancing, where you literally walk around holding someone's hand, so this is absolutely uncharted territory.'

While Greg may be a dance-floor novice, he's hoping his acting skills will help with the performance aspect of the dance – and says his wardrobe makeover will play a part.

'Possibly a saving grace for me is that I could be more dramatic if I can't do the dance,' he says. 'I'm loving the costumes, so I'm looking forward to wearing custom-made, fitted outfits. One of the things about being an actor is you start to inhabit the character as soon as you put on the clothes and the shoes. So I want to push it as far as it goes.'

While Greg is hoping to be the picture of elegance on the floor, he admits to a slight clumsy streak.

'I'm probably most nervous about hurting myself, because I'm very accident prone,' he says. 'Most of my fingers are broken and I tend to fall off things and trip over things, so I've just got to be very aware of that.'

The screen star says he wants to spend as much time as possible in the rehearsal room.

'The more you've come prepared, the more you rehearse, the more opportunity you have for achieving what you want,' he says. 'My aim is to survive as long as possible and do as well as I can. That's how I approach everything. But I'm hoping I can stick around, because I think it's going to be a lot of fun.

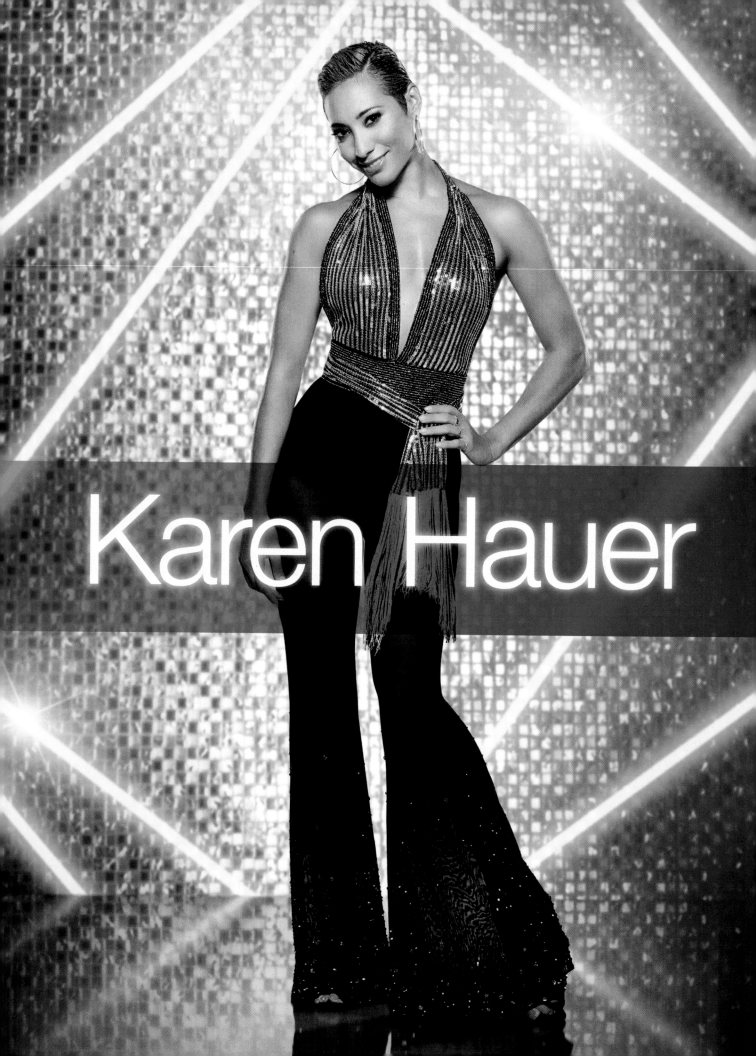

Karen Hauer

Celebrating her tenth *Strictly* series, Karen Hauer is dancing with actor Greg Wise.

The launch show saw the dashing actor arrive on a horse at the Devon house where he filmed *Sense and Sensibility*.

'It was a beautiful country house and the gardens were incredible,' says Karen. 'I felt like I was on a movie set and it was definitely an experience I had never had before. Greg was so excited and he told me he had been hoping for me, which was sweet. He is so excited to learn something new.'

Karen says she will work Greg hard in training but is keen to ensure he has a great time.

'*Strictly* goes by so quickly and sometimes you can get sucked into wanting to reach a certain point, but I want him to always remind himself that this is an experience not many people get to have and to have fun.

'I also told him that I'm about tough love. I am a taskmaster and I think all the pros are. So I told him to be prepared if I get all tough New Yorker on him!'

After his decades on screen, Karen believes Greg's acting experience will be a bonus on the dance floor.

'Acting is one of the hardest things to do, but he won't be afraid to turn into a character, to show emotion and to act the storyline,' she says. 'Physically he's in really good shape and he has a great ballroom frame already. Hopefully, he'll be a jack of all trades, but if he's amazing in ballroom that is exceptional, because that is the hardest thing to be good at.'

Venezuelan-born Karen began dancing at eight, after moving to New York, and won a scholarship to the Martha Graham School of Contemporary Dance two years later. She studied African, contemporary and ballet before moving on to ballroom and Latin at 19. She was World Mambo Champion in 2008 and Rising Star Professional American Rhythm Champion in 2009. She joined *Strictly Come Dancing* in 2012 and last year she reached the Final with *Made in Chelsea* star Jamie Laing.

'It was incredible – I'm still pinching myself,' she says. 'Jamie and I are still such good friends and he texted me at the beginning of this series saying, "I don't want you to get anybody else!"

'Teaching Jamie was like having a puppy. He's adorable. It was wonderful that people were able to discover what a kind and amazing person he is. He was fun to be around, always so positive and full of energy.

'We really loved the Charleston when he was dressed as Hercules, and it still makes me laugh,' she says. 'But our Couple's Choice street dance is hands down the best dance I feel I've done on *Strictly*.'

This year, Anton's move to the judges' desk means Karen is the longest-serving pro dancing in the show, and she says she has learned a lot from her predecessor.

'One of the things that I learned from Anton was that he was always professional, he always had a smile on his face and, although he worked really hard, he took it all in his stride,' she says. 'Everything he did was pretty cool, and everybody respected him. We're all friends and we work as a team and if the younger dancers have any questions about choreography or the show, I'm always happy to give advice. But Anton left me some big shoes to fill!'

Karen is now looking forward to getting back into the rehearsal room to put her new celebrity through his paces.

'I'm excited to teach someone new, to get to know my partner, to create and see how they respond,' she says. 'I'm excited about working with Greg because he has so much experience I can use. I want him to make believe he's Gene Kelly or Fred Astaire and get into his mind that he's playing a character, and I want to inject the love of dance into him.'

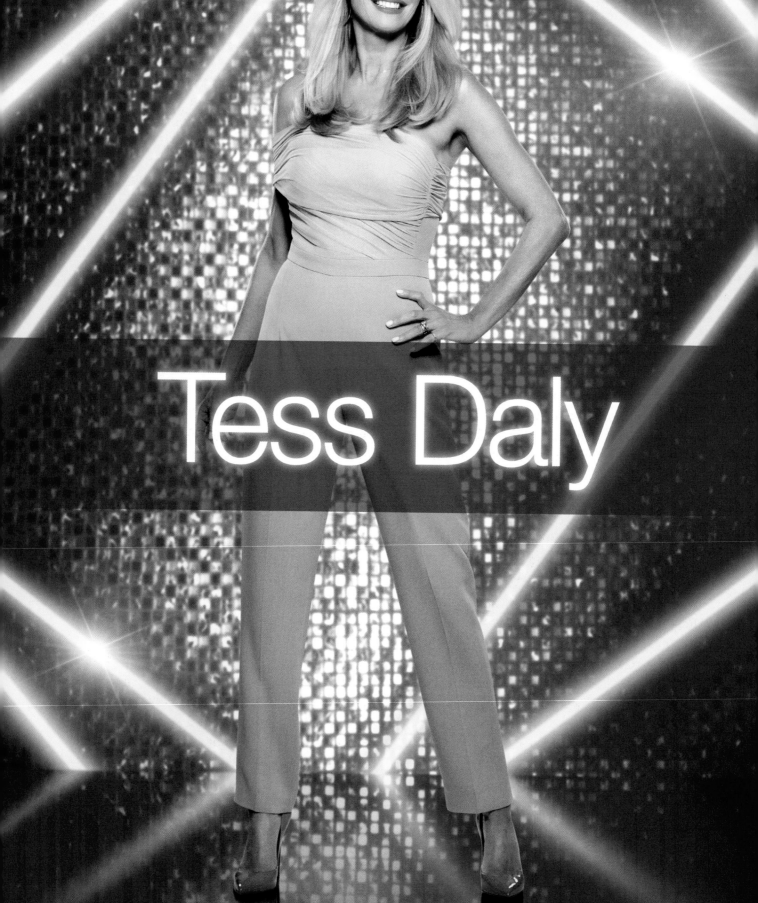

Tess Daly

The glitz and glamour of the *Strictly* studio always puts a spring in the step of host Tess Daly and, as she prepares to preside over her nineteenth battle of the ballroom, she couldn't be more excited.

'This year's intake is a great bunch, with so much personality,' she says. 'They're such an exciting group. I can't wait to see their routines because there are some wonderful dances coming up.'

Having seen the celebrities strut their stuff on the launch show, Tess is already impressed.

'The highlight of the show for me is the group dance, because it's the first time we see them perform and we can check out the potential,' she says. 'What really amazed us all was how close in ability they all are. There are a lot of talented and able dancers from the offset. Of course, it's not always about who's best at the start, but often about who the audience get behind, because they go on a journey of discovery and we watch them grow before our eyes.'

Tess says every one of them has shown a flash of potential on their first outing.

'Adam Peaty did a Latin demo for me, just two steps on the studio floor, and his hips were electric. Rose Ayling-Ellis has a beautiful, enchanting aura about her. There's something elegant and ethereal about her and she'll be compelling to watch. AJ Odudu and Rhys Stephenson have bags of energy and Tilly Ramsay, our youngest, is still only 19 and is so sweet.

'Katie McGlynn is delightful and is finding the prospect of dancing live nerve-wracking, but there are always a lot of nerves on the first night and everyone is so supportive because they are all out of their comfort zone.'

Tess is excited about another *Strictly* first – the all-male partnership of John Whaite and Johannes Radebe.

'John is living his best life and can't get enough of the sequins and spray tan,' she says. 'I think they'll be dynamite, because Johannes is overflowing with creative ideas.'

With three comedians taking to the dance floor, in Nina Wadia, Judi Love and Robert Webb, Tess is expecting some fun-filled routines, too.

'Nina Wadia really stepped up in the group dance and Robert Webb is hilarious in his facial choreography alone. I think he's a real people-pleaser, because he's hysterical to watch. As his famous *Comic Relief* dance in a leotard proved, he is not afraid to let the costumes do the talking.

Although they come from different backgrounds, the class of '21 are already a close-knit gang.

'There's a camaraderie, which is great,' says Tess. 'At the launch show, they were cheering each other on and there was a lot of whooping and hollering. They're so supportive, because in *Strictly* you're thrown in at the deep end and it's a bonding experience.'

This year, Tess is looking forward to the themed weeks – Movie Week, Musicals Week and Halloween.

'That's *Strictly* at its best,' she says. 'The hair and make-up and costume departments are incredible, and they can show off their skills to the max. Halloween is a highlight because I love to see everybody getting into character.'

As a *Strictly* original, Tess is the perfect person to give the new contestants a tip or two – and she advises taking a leaf out of champion Bill Bailey's book.

'They've got to do everything their pro partner tells them and throw themselves into it,' she says. 'At last year's launch show, nobody would have picked Bill Bailey as the eventual winner, but we watched him grow in strength, confidence and ability. He's the prime example of someone fully embracing the concept, committing and working hard. The more you embrace it and let go of your inhibitions, the more the viewers at home enjoy it with you.'

Do You Know Your Pros?

Our fabulous dancers have us all in a twirl every Saturday night, but how well do you know the pros? Here are a few clues to each dancer. See if you can identify all of them in our fun quiz.

1. The longest-serving female pro, having joined the show in 2012. Originally from Venezuela, she is a keen baker and dog lover, with three pooches at home.

2. Born in Sicily, this dancer has a tattoo that reads 'Born to Win'. He holds the Guinness World Record for Jive kicks and flicks.

3. Studied civil engineering before becoming a dancer and has lived in Germany, where she appeared as a pro on *Let's Dance*.

4. Originally from the Ukraine, she is a two-time World and European Champion in Ballroom & Latin 'Ten' Dance.

5. Born on an army base in Germany, he has represented Finland, the Netherlands and the UK during the course of his competitive career.

6. The former Italian Latin Champion has also represented Belgium in competition. He has a bull tattooed on his chest.

7. Born in Russia, she worked as an Assistant Choreographer on *Strictly* for two years before taking an on-camera role in 2018.

8. Nineteen times Slovenian Ballroom & Latin Champion, this dancer won the glitterball trophy in his first year of *Strictly*, in 2013, dancing with a model.

9. Former British National Champion who began dancing at the age of eight. She danced with JJ Chalmers in series 18.

10. This Spanish dancer first appeared on *Strictly* in series 14, partnering Tameka Empson.

11. Danced from the age of five and won the adult New Vogue WA Championship with brother Andrew. Danced with Robbie Savage in the 2017 Christmas special.

12. This dancer was the Amateur Latin Champion of China and starred in *Burn the Floor* before joining *Strictly* in 2019.

13. Double finalist in the South African version of *Strictly* before joining the UK team in 2018. His first celeb partner was Catherine Tyldesley.

14. Russian born and once trained by Karen Hardy. Last year she became the first pro to dance in a same-sex couple with a celebrity.

Karen Hauer

Giovanni Pernice

Oti Mabuse

Nadiya Bychkova

Neil Jones

Graziano Di Prima

Luba Mushtuk

Answers

8 Aljaž Škorjanec

Amy Dowden **9**

10 Gorka Márquez

Dianne Buswell **11**

12 Nancy Xu

Johannes Radebe **13**

14 Katya Jones

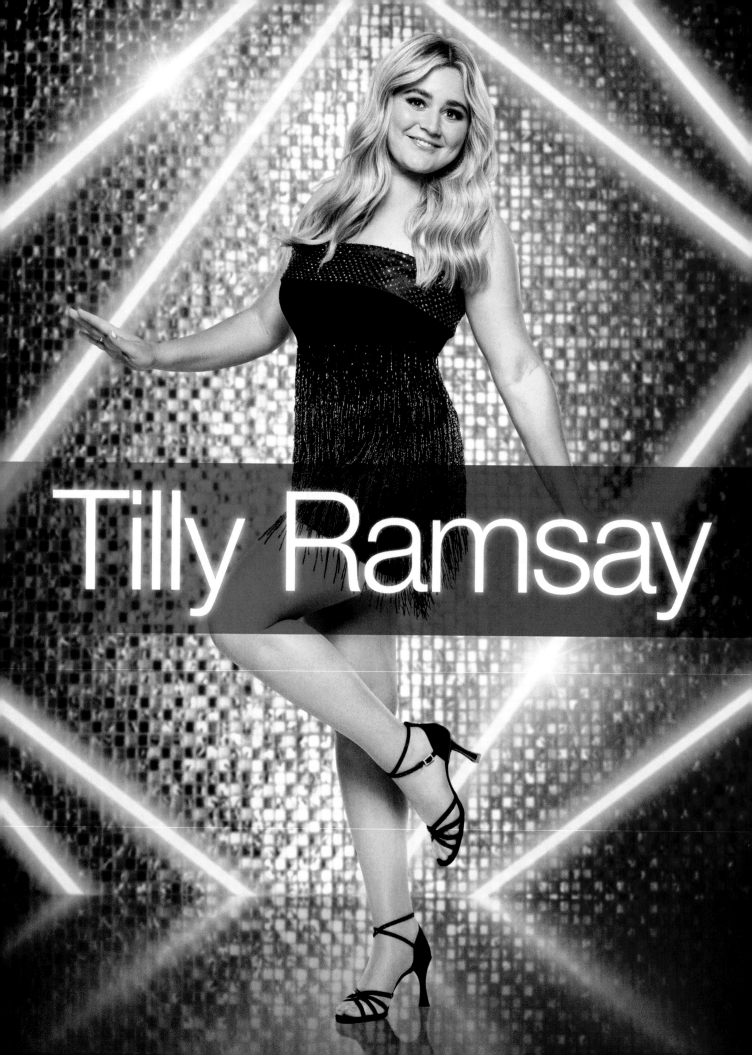

Tilly Ramsay

TV chef and social media star Tilly Ramsay is hoping to cook up a storm on the dance floor and is most looking forward to performing an elegant Waltz. But first she'll have to get used to her new dancing shoes.

'I hate wearing heels,' she explains. 'I've only worn them once in my life, to my eighteenth birthday party, and they were off within five minutes. They were too painful. I never put them back on, until recently, when I've been walking around the house in heels to get used to them. After a couple of minutes, my feet hurt and my slippers come back on. I'd love to be able to do the Waltz in slippers!'

Tilly is looking forward to embracing the glamorous *Strictly* style even if it is a far cry from her usual casual look.

'I'm very excited because it's a big change for me,' she says. 'The hair and make-up is going to be pretty cool. I'm used to falling out of bed and just going about my day, so having make-up and my hair styled will be great. I'm definitely going to embrace the sequins.'

The daughter of chef Gordon Ramsay, Tilly has grown up around cooking and made her first TV appearance at the age of four. At 14, she landed her own TV show and has appeared alongside dad Gordon too. Now Tilly says Gordon and mum Tana will be cheering her on during her *Strictly* journey.

'Mum and Dad are both excited for me but also nervous because they know that I'm feeling slightly terrified,' she says. 'My family have all been brilliant, apart from my brother, who said, "Why? You can't dance." Thank you for the confidence boost – that's just what I needed!

'Dad is very excited because he's always wanted to learn how to dance, but he's definitely got two left feet. I will try to teach him some moves, but I do get slightly impatient with him because it takes him a very long time.'

Although Tilly has posted short dance clips on social media, she says she rates her dancing skills as 'very, very low'.

'I really am not very good at dancing,' she laughs. 'Mum tried to get us into ballet when we were young, but I wasn't very good so I ended up in football camp with my brother.'

Tilly, who will be starting her first year at university during her *Strictly* run, is the youngest contestant at 19, but she says growing up in the Ramsay household has prepared her for the judges' comments.

'I think I'll take feedback from the judges pretty well because I live with one of the harshest critics there is – my dad,' she laughs. 'But it's all about learning and you need constructive criticism to improve.'

Ahead of her dance-floor debut, Tilly has been getting some useful tips from former *Strictly* contestants and says she can't wait to 'throw myself in the deep end'.

'I've had a few bits of advice,' she says. 'Ruth Langsford told me to wear blister plasters before you get blisters. But most people have just said that it's such a great show to take part in and just to have fun and enjoy it.

'I can't wait to throw myself into this big challenge, because it's something that's really out of my comfort zone. But it will be so cool to learn how to dance.

'My mum's a big fan of *Strictly* and she got us into it when we were very young. Our treat on a Saturday was to stay up and watch the live show. It doesn't feel real, being on it, and I'm so excited for this amazing opportunity.'

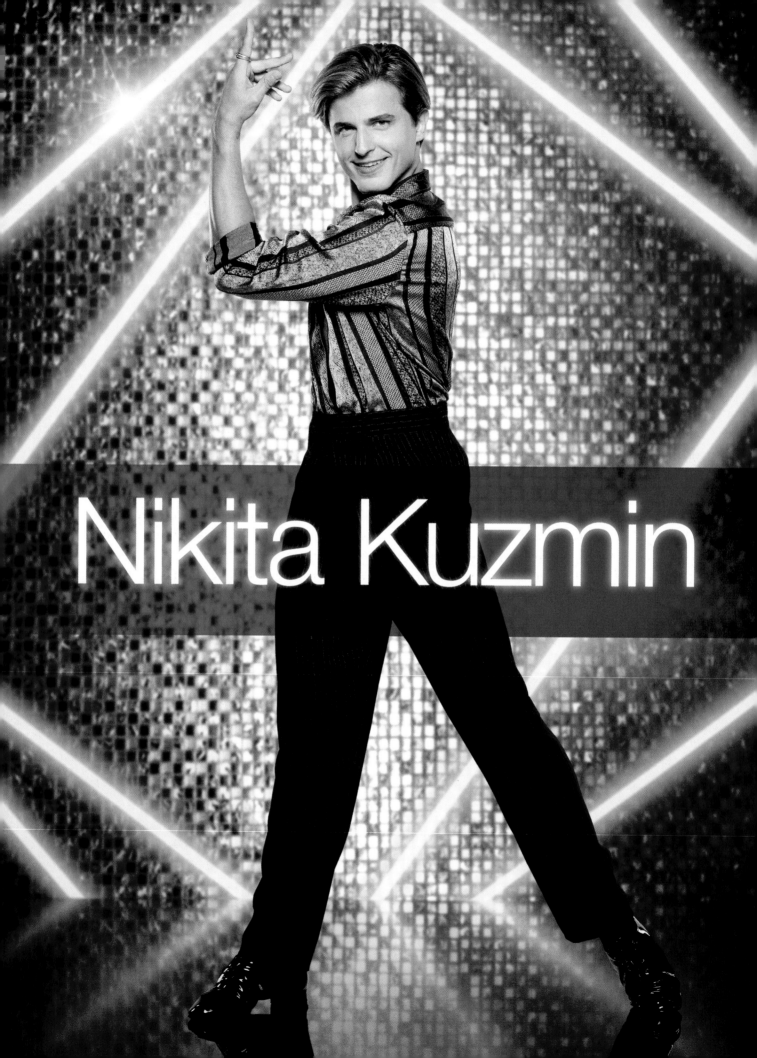

Nikita Kuzmin

Newcomer Nikita Kuzmin is thrilled to be dancing with TV chef Tilly Ramsay on his debut year, and is hoping their pairing will be a recipe for success.

'I'm extremely happy and very excited to be on *Strictly*, especially now I'm starting to train with Tilly,' he says. 'We get along so well together, and we've been having a good time so far. We're laughing all the time, and in the first days of training she showed me that she wants to go for it and work hard. That's all I could wish for in a partner. I will do my best to bring her that glitterball and I'm sure that Tilly wants the same.'

The 23-year-old dancer and choreographer says his new pupil is showing a lot of promise in the early days.

'I think Tilly has the potential to be very good,' he says. 'She has the determination – what I would call tiger eyes – and she has sparkle. She has such grace and the beauty of movement already naturally in her. I know she's really looking forward to the Waltz, but I think she'll be good in both ballroom and Latin.'

Nikita says his teaching style is simultaneously tough and kind.

'I'm usually very strict,' he says. 'I go by the rule that if you do something, you do it 100 per cent, so while you practise you give it your all, and when there's a break you commit to that too and have a laugh.'

Born in Ukraine, Nikita started dancing at four when he failed the entrance to karate club because he couldn't do a forward roll! 'My mother always loved Latin American music, so she brought first my sister Anastasia, then me, to the dance classes. We have never looked back since.' At the tender age of nine, Nikita moved to Italy and continued to study dance, becoming six-time Latin and Ballroom National Champion. While his sister is a pro on the Italian *Dancing with the Stars,* Nikita has been living in Germany, where he appeared on *Let's Dance*. When he got the call for *Strictly*, he says he was so shocked that he couldn't tell anyone for an hour and a half.

'It was such a dream come true, I didn't know what to do and how to act,' he says. 'When it finally sunk in, I called my mother and she screamed down the phone!'

As a new recruit, Nikita says he has been welcomed into the *Strictly* fold with open arms.

'The pros have all been so helpful, giving me advice and helping me out whenever there was something I didn't know about the show,' he says. 'It was the best welcome I could have got. The group rehearsals went so well and the routines are unbelievable – I cannot wait till everybody can see them. Obviously, we have amazing choreographers and amazing professionals and the whole group came together so well.'

Despite Tilly's dad Gordon having a fearsome reputation, Nikita says he has also been welcomed by the TV chef.

'We have spoken a couple of times on video call and he's actually lovely,' he says. 'I had it in my imagination that he would be scary, but he's been very supportive, and Tilly is wonderful. I'm pretty sure everything is going to be beautiful.'

Bursting with enthusiasm, Nikita says he can't wait for all the new experiences on *Strictly*.

'I'm looking forward to the first show, before we start to dance, when the announcer calls our names and we're maybe a little nervous but excited to perform,' he says. 'I'm really looking forward to all the first moments: the first comments from the judges, the first dance. I also can't wait to see the progress, see a smile on Tilly's face. It's one of the best things when you see people who didn't know how to dance starting to coordinate and move with the music. It's just beautiful.'

Strictly Quiz

Are you a *Strictly* superfan with an encyclopaedic knowledge of the show? Put your memory to the test with our fun quiz – and mind you don't miss a step.

1 What year did *Strictly* first burst onto our TV screens?

2 Who was the first male celebrity to win the glitterball?

3 Which reality star injured himself in 2019 but returned a year later and made it to the Final?

4 Whose opening Cha-cha-cha in series 18 was described by Craig as 'like dancing on hot coals after a dozen double espressos'?

5 Oti Mabuse is one of two pros to have won the series glitterball twice. Name the other one.

6 As a dancer, judge Shirley Ballas specialised in which area of dance, earning her a special nickname?

7 Who stepped into the judge's chair for two weeks in series 18?

8 In which country did the Rumba and Cha-cha-cha originate?

9 Which celebrity danced their Final showdance to 'Boogie Wonderland' by Earth, Wind & Fire in series 18?

10 Who climbed out of a coffin for her series 9 Rumba on Halloween?

11 Name the only model to walk away with the glitterball.

12 Which boyband star bagged the trophy in the 2018 Christmas special?

13 In 2013, *Strictly* moved to Elstree Studios – but where was it filmed beforehand?

14 Which dance, performed each year on *Strictly*, originated in the African-American clubs of the 1920s and came to the UK with the American GIs in the 1930s?

15 In which year was the Couple's Choice introduced to *Strictly*?

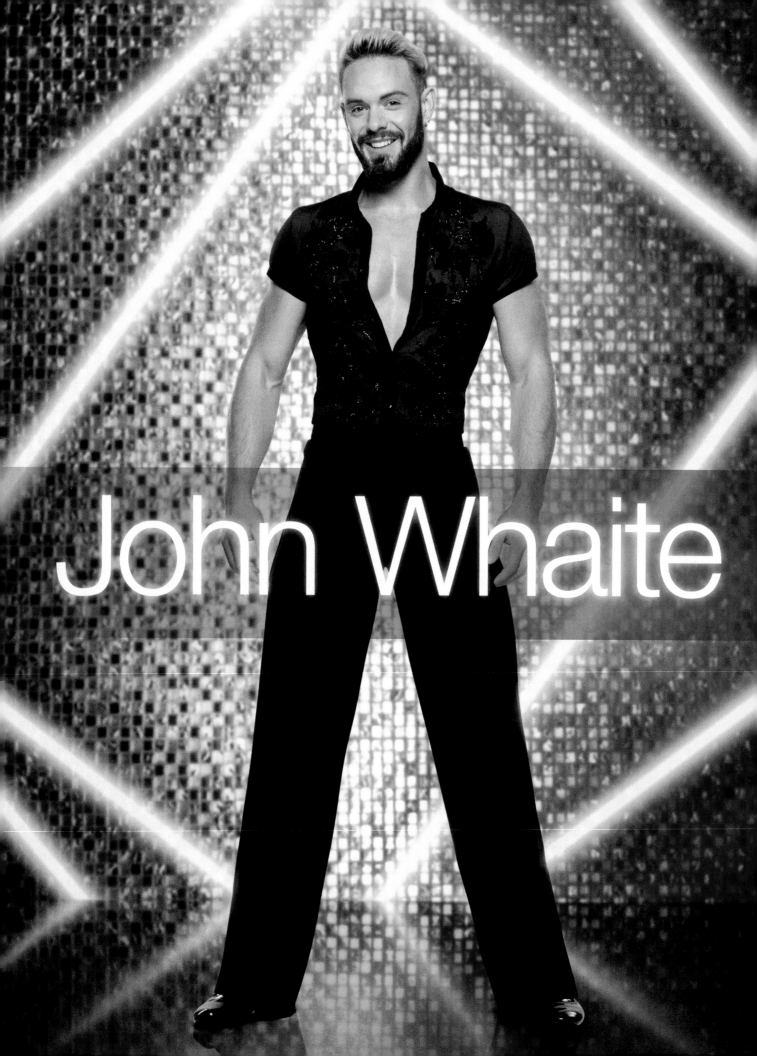

John Whaite

Chef and TV presenter John Whaite will be whisking up a whirlwind on the *Strictly* dance floor this series and is looking forward to bringing sparkle into the viewers' living room every night.

'I have been obsessed with glitter and sequins since I was a baby,' he says. 'When I got offered *Strictly*, I was honoured because the show brings joy and razzmatazz into everyone's life, and I have wanted to do it since I was a boy.'

John is also proud to be half of the first all-male partnership in the competition.

'The reaction has been so positive,' he says. 'I can honestly say I haven't had a single message of negativity. My name was announced by Matt Lucas on Radio 2 and, when we were talking I realised how important a step forward this is, for kids who watch the show to have same-sex role models.'

John was raised on a Lancashire farm and gained a first-class degree in law at Manchester University. But in 2012, his career took an unexpected turn when he won *The Great British Bake Off*. He has now published five cookbooks and become a TV favourite, bagging a regular slot on *Steph's Packed Lunch*.

Although John says his current dance skills are usually only showcased in nightclubs, he is confident he can pick up the choreography.

'I'm one of those people who has to be shown what to do, but if I watch things, I pick them up quite quickly,' he says. 'I'm just hoping that my old hips don't give up on me. I've been rubbing WD-40 on them for the past few weeks, trying to limber them up!'

The cake king is hoping Latin will be his recipe for success but says getting the facial expressions could be the sticking point.

'I want to learn an intense Samba and really go for it. If I'm thinking about the steps, I wonder if I may have a blank look of concentration on my face,' he says.

'I'm more nervous about the ballroom dances. In the Latin, you can add a shimmy and some sass and get those hips moving. To keep my shoulders back and my back straight in the ballroom dances will be more difficult.'

While learning to dance is the main objective for John, getting the *Strictly* makeover is the icing on the cake.

'I'm looking forward to the spray tans, I'm not going to lie,' he jokes. 'I want to be as glamorous as possible. Vicky Gill and her wardrobe team are absolutely incredible, so I'm looking forward to wearing beautiful clothes with sequins, glitter and a lot of jazziness.'

Despite John's baking prowess, fellow contestants and pros hoping for sweet treats backstage are going to be sadly disappointed, as he is hanging up his apron for the show's duration.

'I've made a vow not to make any cakes during *Strictly* because I can't take the pressure of the other celebs judging my cakes as well as the judges judging my dancing!'

John is keen to put in the hours in rehearsal, adding, 'I don't have an off switch.' But he has a canine pal who will be keeping him grounded.

'If I wake up in the night with anxiety, I get my dog, Abel, and put him on my bed, stroking him and talking to him,' he says. 'So if I feel anxious on the show I will look at pictures of my dog. Luckily my partner, Paul, and my dog are moving down to London with me for the series, so at the end of the day I will go home, cook my own tea and do my own washing, and that way I'll keep my feet on the ground.'

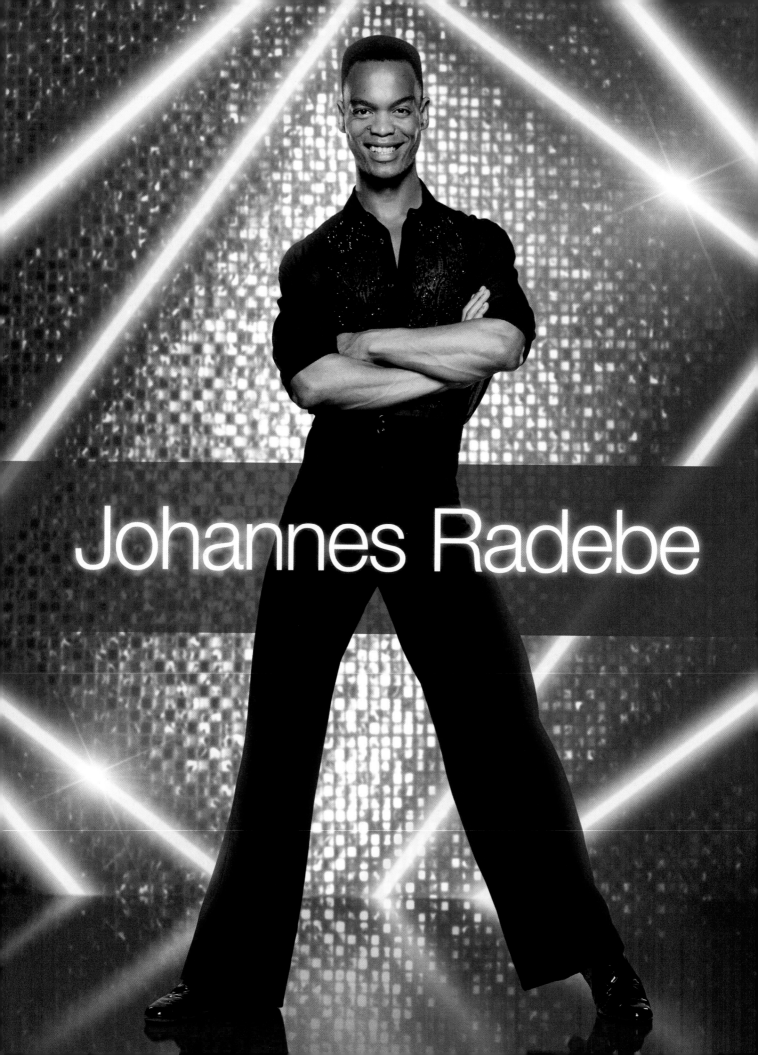

Johannes Radebe

South African star Johannes Radebe is over the moon to be dancing with John Whaite in the first all-male partnership to compete for the glitterball. And he's hoping to stir things up on the dance floor with the former *Great British Bake Off* winner.

'I'm beside myself with joy,' he says. 'When John was announced, I hoped he would be my celebrity partner, so it feels wonderful. When we met for the reveal at his house he was really happy, too. We are both gay men and I understand where he's coming from because it's a lived experience. We both know what this means to us, and our community at large, and we are excited for what this partnership can be.'

As soon as the pair met, baker John was keen to tell his new teacher he was ready to throw himself into the mix.

'John asked me how many hours I like to practise and said, "I'm available from nine to five, or whatever it takes." I was just taken aback because it's such a welcome surprise. He knows what he needs to do and that's so refreshing. Also, in our first day of rehearsal he seemed to get the steps down really quickly.'

Johannes is looking forward to getting creative with his choreography and says that dancing with a male partner means he can play around with the traditional lead-and-follow rules.

'The fact that we can reverse roles and play around is where the beauty and the power is going to come from,' he says. 'The versatility is going to be the beautiful thing about this partnership and allows me to be more creative.'

Partnering one of the UK's most talented bakers also brings other advantages – and training is always improved by the prospect of cake.

'John quizzed me about what I eat, my nutrition and so on, and I think he's concerned about me because, as a dancer, I'm into my salads, trying to maintain a shape,' laughs Johannes. 'He said he was going to have to start feeding me up. He's promised to bring some cake in, which is great, and he's already brought brownies!'

Born in Zamdela Sasolburg, in South Africa, Johannes began learning dance at seven and competed in provincial Latin competitions. At 20, he joined the Afro Arimba Dance Company and has since become two-time Professional South African Latin Champion and three-time South African Amateur Latin Champion. He joined the South African version of *Strictly Come Dancing* in 2014, twice making the Grand Final, before joining the UK show, and last year he danced with actress Caroline Quentin.

'With Caroline, I laughed so much and it was amazing,' he says. 'We took the show seriously, but we allowed ourselves to enjoy the process. I can't tell you the laughs we had and that's what I will always remember about the partnership.'

The latest intake of celebrity recruits has made an impression on Johannes already, and he says it will be a great year for *Strictly*.

'I feel like the class of 2021 are all eager beavers and it's beautiful because they all really want to be a part of the show,' he says. 'You can see it in the way they move, in the way they hold themselves. Everybody's taking it very seriously.'

Despite the high standard of the competition, Johannes is hoping that getting to the Final with John will be a piece of cake.

'I would love to take John to the Final of *Strictly Come Dancing* and it would be a first for me in the United Kingdom,' he says. 'I want to have an opportunity to dance every single style with him, to do all the Latin and ballroom dances and our Couple's Choice. That would be amazing.'

Pro Pep Talks

Taking to the *Strictly* dance floor may be out of some celebrities' comfort zones, but the professional dancers are with their partners every step of the way.

As well as being brilliant teachers, they are fantastic at offering the right encouragement and giving their pupils a confidence boost before each live performance. Here, some of the pros share the secrets of their pre-show pep talks.

ALJAŽ ŠKORJANEC

For me, the most important time in every routine is the first five seconds of rehearsal. I always start the day with a hug and tell my celebrity, 'We're going to have the best day ever,' because I like to start positive.

If I see my partner losing energy or concentration, I make sure they take a break. When you have a head that's too full, it's the worst time to learn something. So I always give people space to collect themselves and their thoughts, and when we get back to it they will learn quicker.

Before we hit the dance floor on Saturday night, I say to my partner, 'Trust yourself. You know the steps and I can't wait to dance with you on that floor.'

LUBA MUSHTUK

I tell my celebrity partner, 'You're doing this for you, so just enjoy it. I've got your back. I'm here for you every step of the way.' If they are nervous about the live performance, I tell them, 'Look at me, it's just you and me dancing. We can do this and we will. I know you can do it because I've seen you, so just go out there and give it your all. I'm so proud of you, no matter what happens.'

GIOVANNI PERNICE

When I first meet my celebrity I talk to them to make sure they feel comfortable with me, and ease them into the steps slowly.

Once I know them better, I choreograph a routine that suits them and that they feel confident performing, which is important. Before we hit the floor on Saturday night, I tell them they are amazing. Confidence is crucial.

GORKA MÁRQUEZ

This is one of my favourite parts of *Strictly*. You are a mentor to your celebrity partner, and it is not just about teaching them a dance; it's much more than that. Every individual is different and that's the beauty of it. The professionals need to get to know that person and how to approach them to get the best out of them. From day one, I like to know their reason for doing the show. Knowing their WHY is very important, as that will help me to understand how I should approach them and how far I can push them.

On studio days, I try to keep them away from the noise around the show as much as possible and create a bubble to keep them calm and focused on the dance. When it is time to get on the dance floor, I tell them not to worry about anything, to forget about everything around them and think they are alone with me in the rehearsal studio. It is only 90 seconds, and they will never have to dance that again so make the most of it, enjoy it and have fun! My most important thing to tell them, for the whole show, is to enjoy every single day as it comes. Each week might be your last one, so make the most of this wonderful life experience. You won't regret anything if you give it your everything.

KAREN HAUER

I'm very encouraging and I like to push the limits with my celebrities, and make them feel like they're in good hands, and that they can trust me. I work on building their confidence and I want them to be comfortable.

Before the routine on a Saturday night, I always tell my partner, 'You can do this. Enjoy the moment.'

The audience only sees the routine on that day and I've been there the whole week, seeing how hard my celebrity has worked. I will always say, 'You're brilliant at what you're doing. This is for you, for your body, for your mind and for your fans.'

DIANNE BUSWELL

When I'm prepping my celebrity for the live Saturday night, I think it's so important to encourage them as much as possible. It can be easy for them to forget that dancing at this level takes years of training and comes as second nature to us professionals, but it's completely new to them. Patience, support and belief is everything, so before taking to the floor, I remind my partner that they have done all the hard work during the week. I tell them, 'You know it. Don't overthink it, just enjoy it!' The results show can be more nerve-racking than the live show. If that red light shines down on you, sure, it's disappointing, but I reassure them that I'm right there with them and that it's another chance to dance and possibly stay in the competition.

Again, in that moment, you have to encourage as much as possible and try not to let your partner overthink it – enjoy the moment.

NEIL JONES

On day one, we start by listening to the music and understanding the rhythm. Straight after that I teach them the whole routine and it doesn't matter if they can dance it or not, just that they know what to expect and we know if we need to make changes. By the end of the day, they know what is happening and they can feel relaxed.

On the day of the show I always make sure I am there for my partner whenever they need to practise or just have a chat, so they can feel relaxed. I tell them it doesn't matter what happens on the night as long as they have fun and enjoy every moment, because I am really proud of what they have accomplished over the week.

Straight after we have performed I tell them, 'Think about how you danced and what you have been able to do in the past week. Tomorrow is your day off, so get some rest because it's back to working hard again on Monday.'

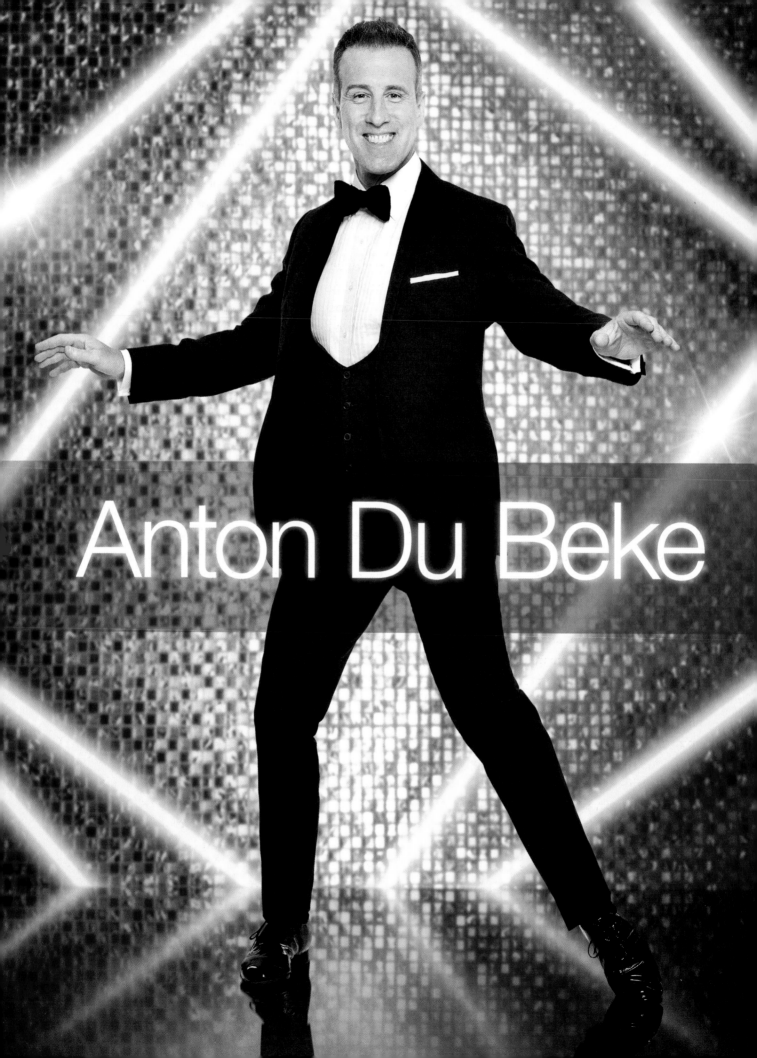

As *Strictly*'s longest-serving pro, Anton Du Beke has been entertaining viewers since the first series burst onto the nation's screens.

But this series, he's joining the judges' panel alongside Shirley, Craig and Motsi, and says his own experience as a dancer on the show gives him a unique perspective.

'I'm very excited,' he says. 'I can't wait to get going. Having done it as a professional, I know exactly what each couple and each professional is trying to do and I'm looking forward to seeing if what they try to achieve develops over the weeks.

'Not being under one of the spotlights in the results show will be wonderful, and I'm really looking forward to having something to do in the Final!'

A promising footballer and boxer, Anton joined his local dancing school in Sevenoaks, Kent, at the age of 14, after he was sent to meet his sister from her class. A huge fan of Fred Astaire, he began specialising in ballroom at 17 and competing as an amateur, funding his training with a series of day jobs. He began dancing with partner Erin Boag in 1997 and the pair went on to win many national and international awards before being snapped up by *Strictly Come Dancing* in 2004. Over 18 series, he performed unforgettable numbers with such celebrity partners as Ann Widdecombe, Judy Murray and Nancy Dell'Olio. In 2019, he made it to the Final with actress Emma Barton.

Having spent two weeks as a guest judge last year, he promises that his experience as a professional dancer on the show will make him a 'kinder' judge. And viewers will still be treated to flashes of that famous Anton humour.

'I have empathy for the professionals and an understanding that what comes out on Saturday night isn't always exactly what they've been working towards during the week. It can turn out differently or doesn't quite come off the way you're hoping, so I'll take that into consideration. All the couples are trying their best and that's all you can do. It will be constructive criticism with a smile!'

Having been on the receiving end of Craig Revel Horwood's sharp tongue in the past, Anton is hoping for fireworks at the desk.

'I hope I have a few disagreements with Craig because that will make it more interesting,' he jokes. 'I'll be mortified if I have to agree with him every five minutes.'

While Anton couldn't be happier to be switching roles, he admits he has experienced the odd pang over the group dance rehearsals and the first week of the show.

'The week the pros meet their celebrities is such an exciting week and I know how they'll all be feeling. They're all going to be excited and eager to get started, and the celebrities will be nervous and unsure of what's going to happen. Also, we have four new pros who are on the show for the first time, which is exciting, and the celebrity line-up is a tremendous group of people. It's going to be a fabulous, fun year.'

Since his first show, when he stepped onto the dance floor with singer Lesley Garrett, Anton has watched *Strictly* evolve and he thinks it's now bigger and better than ever.

'We get a new cast of celebrities every year, which makes each series fresh,' he says. 'But also, subtle changes in production make it the huge show it is today. Plus, viewers still love the live music, the *Strictly* singers and the musical acts, and they love the professionals and watching them do their thing.

'*Strictly Come Dancing* is so multi-layered, and it keeps getting better and better. This year's going to be a beauty.'

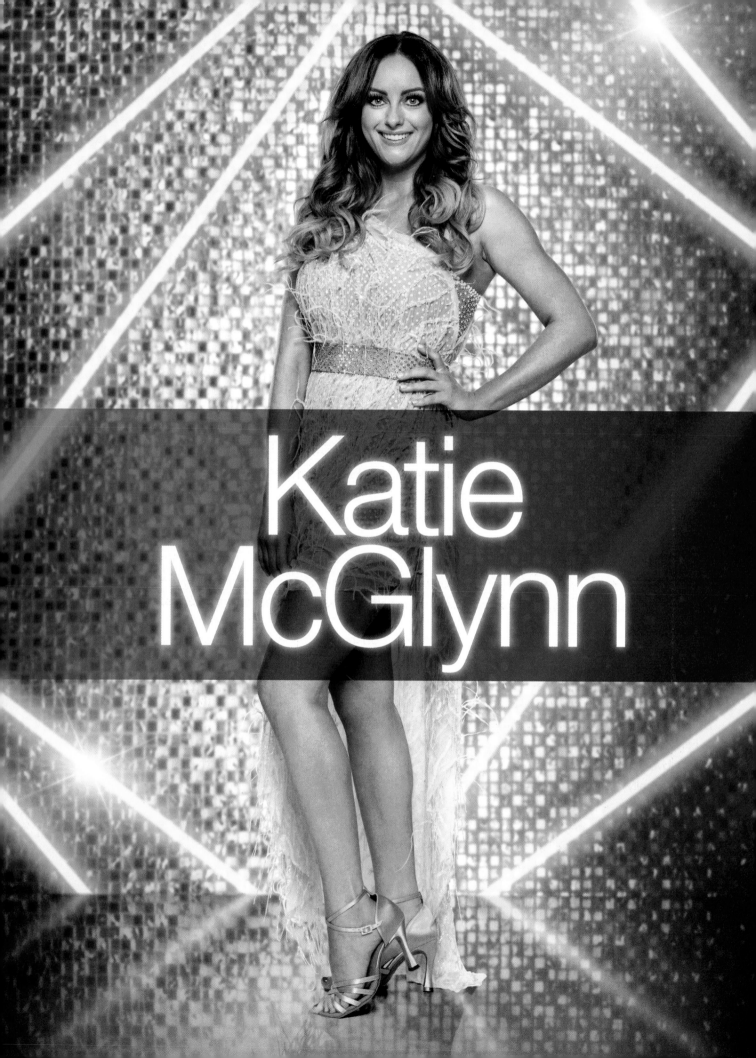

Katie
McGlynn

Actress Katie McGlynn is a huge *Strictly* fan and says signing up for the show was a secret ambition she had held for years.

'I watch it every year and I'm always flabbergasted at how much fun the contestants have,' she says. 'So when the opportunity arose this year, it was a dream come true. I cannot wait to get *Strictly*-fied and I can't wait to try my hand at dancing because I have no idea what I'm doing.'

The former *Coronation Street* actress, currently starring in *Hollyoaks*, has had sound advice from pals who have already taken on the *Strictly* challenge.

'My former *Corrie* co-star Catherine Tyldesley told me, "Remember that you're going to know the routine by Friday and Saturday. It doesn't feel like you will at the beginning, but it all comes together, so relax and enjoy it." My friend Lisa Riley said to "be yourself – as daft as a brush", because it's a fun, relaxed show and that suits my personality.'

Manchester-born Katie got her first major acting role at 16 in *Waterloo Road*, and went on to star as Sinead Tinker in *Coronation Street* for seven years. Her tragic storyline, which saw the young mum die from cancer in 2020, moved the nation to tears, but Katie is hoping viewers will now see her lighter side.

'I love doing challenging storylines, but I am normally a positive, fun person,' she says. 'I always find the funny side and try to laugh instead of getting upset when bad things happen, so this is my cup of tea all over. I want to smile, I want to laugh, I want to dance, have a good time and hopefully make some lifelong friends along the way.'

Katie's sense of humour clearly runs in the family, as she got a mixed response when she announced her news at home.

'My family's reaction was all positive, but my dad started laughing and said, "Katie, please don't fall over," because I am so clumsy,' she says. 'My dad's going to be laughing throughout the whole routine, thinking I'm going to make a mistake or fall, because I'm not an elegant person. But they can't wait, they're very excited.'

While her default look is a beaming smile, the 28-year-old is looking forward to taking on more fiery characters for the dramatic dances.

'I'm very excited to learn the Paso Doble because it's such a passionate, moody dance, which I think I'll really enjoy,' she says. 'For the sensual dances, like the Rumba, I'm going to have to morph into a different character, because I'm just not sexy. I'm quite an awkward person. Also, I'm slightly daunted by the really fast ones, like the Jive and the Quickstep, because of the speedy footwork.'

As a fan, Katie says she's excited to meet the judges and says she's most looking forward to the moment at the end of the routine.

'I can't wait for the feeling of relief when you come off the dance floor, you've done the best dance that you could and you nailed the steps,' she says. 'I hope that's going to happen. Because I'm an actor, I love that feeling when I have just come offstage and everything has gone the way it was supposed to. Someone should put that in a bottle.'

The accomplished actress is also looking forward to being dressed to the nines for each performance.

'I'm hoping I'll stay in until Halloween, because dressing up and going out for Halloween is my favourite thing to do,' she says. 'But I'm looking forward to all the dresses. As soon as I get my fake tan on, and all the sequins, I will be ready and I'll feel like a princess.'

Gorka Márquez

After making it to the Final with *EastEnder* Maisie Smith in series 18, Spanish dancer Gorka Márquez is back with another soap queen on his arm, in the shape of *Coronation Street* and *Hollyoaks* star Katie McGlynn.

The dance partners were paired on a rooftop in Katie's home town of Manchester, which is now Gorka's adopted home.

'I think it's going to be a great partnership,' he says. 'I can't wait to start working with Katie and get on that dance floor. Katie is a lovely girl, very chilled, very laid-back, a proper Mancunian. I love that we're both from Manchester. We have the same accent so there is no problem with the language barriers!'

After the rooftop reveal at the city's landmark 20 Stories, Gorka told his new partner he was aiming high.

'When she first saw me, I don't know if Katie was excited or scared, but I think she was excited!' he says. 'I told her that I hope I can help her to make it all the way to the Final, but obviously I want her to have fun. However far we get, she will always remember the show as having the best time ever.'

Talented Latin champ Gorka has already got some ideas for a move or two and is hoping to incorporate Katie's ideas.

'I asked her what her signature move was, and she said it was the shimmy, so we may have plenty of shimmying on the show,' he says. 'It's too soon to say whether she will be suited more to the Latin or ballroom. Katie thinks she will like the Latin dances more, but in my experience, a lot of people say they will be better at Latin or ballroom and then end up loving the other one. So we'll wait and see.'

Gorka is hoping that, like Masie before her, Katie's acting skills can come to the fore on the dance floor.

'When it comes to the dance and the performance on Saturday night, acting plays a very big role and is a great strength to have,' he explains. 'Knowing that she can think about it as being a character in the dance will be very helpful and we can build stories within the dance, which will help her to play the roles. Being an actress helped Maisie a lot, so it will be a very positive thing for Katie to have.'

Born in Bilbao, Spain, Gorka took up dancing at the age of 11 and represented his country in the World Latin Championships in 2010 and the Semi-finals of the 2012 World DanceSport Federation World Cup. Gorka joined the *Strictly* family in 2016, partnering *EastEnders* star Tameka Empson. He was a Finalist with Alexandra Burke in 2017, danced with Katie Piper in 2018, and last year narrowly missed out on the glitterball with Maisie, after a spectacular journey to the Final.

'The whole series was incredible,' he says. 'I loved every single second and Maisie was such a fun person. She was the perfect student. She was talented and capable of doing anything she wanted to do. She worked hard and trusted me 100 per cent from day one.

'We had so much fun dancing together. Every day in rehearsals, we couldn't stop laughing but always we got the job done. Even if she was busy with work, she always came into training with a smile – she was amazing.'

Now he has his eyes on the Final again, and he's looking forward to seeing Katie strut her stuff on the dance floor.

'As a pro dancer you always want to enjoy the relationship with your partner and have the best time, because we're going to spend a lot of hours dancing together. So I'm looking forward to having a laugh, creating great numbers and hopefully making people fall in love with us as a partnership and want to support us so we can make it all the way to the end!'

Claudia Winkleman

Presenter Claudia Winkleman is full of anticipation for the new series of *Strictly*, and while she loves every minute of the competition, it's the first meeting of the dancers, celebrities and crew that she most looks forward to.

'The first time we're all in the studio is unbelievably thrilling and goosebump-inducing,' she says. 'I can't wait for us all to be together. The first group dance with the celebrities is always tremendous, because you can see in their faces that either they're terrified or they're thinking, "Hold on, this is a laugh." They always feel slightly wobbly, until they're paired up with a partner, but once they're a little team, they feel so much better. So my advice when I first meet them will be to hold steady until you get your partner and also just to enjoy it. I'll tell them they are in the hands of the best hair and make-up team, the best costume team and the best production team, so just to throw themselves in.'

Claudia, who has been co-presenting with Tess Daly since 2014, is looking forward to meeting the new intake and says it looks like a bumper year for fun.

'I say this every year, but I think this group is the best ever,' she says. 'I can't wait to meet them all. I've met Robert Webb because I hosted *Let's Dance for Comic Relief* when he did his *Flashdance* routine and it blew our minds, so I cannot wait to see him on the dance floor again. I met Judi Love once, briefly, and I loved her, and it's brilliant to have Adam Peaty, straight from his Olympic triumph. As per usual, the booking team have done an amazing job and picked such a fantastic group. I cannot wait to spend time with all of them.'

Aged from 19 to 55, the new celebs are a wide-ranging group, but Claudia says taking part in *Strictly* helps form a bond like no other show.

'They are already mixing so well,' says Claudia. '*Strictly* stars always do, because they're experiencing something so extraordinary and the only other people who are going through the same thing are their fellow contestants, so they look after each other. I meet past contestants all the time that still message, have dinner together and even go on holiday. It's lovely.'

After years of chatting to Anton Du Beke in her Clauditorium, the host is thrilled to see him on the judges' panel.

'Anton is the perfect choice,' she says. 'He was brilliant when he stood in before and he's a lovely man. He's been there since the beginning, and I think he'll be kind and constructive. He'll be able to say, "I know what's happened there. Why don't you do it this way?" The dancers love him, so they'll really appreciate and respect everything he has to say, as they do with the other three. It's a great panel of four, even though we will miss Bruno.'

As the original presenter of *It Takes Two*, Claudia is also giving her seal of approval to former pro Janette Manrara, who is taking over hosting duties from Zoe Ball.

'We'll miss Zoe, but Janette will be perfect,' she says. 'She's got all the knowledge and all the personality. She is our pocket rocket and she's going to smash it.'

Last year's series, which saw Bill Bailey clinch the title, was 'really special', says Claudia, and she particularly loved the show-stopping Final.

'It was a magical year, and all the contestants just threw themselves into it,' she says. 'It felt like we were in an extraordinary snow globe, and Bill and Oti's showdance to 'The Show Must Go On' was a moment I will never forget. It was one of my all-time favourites.

'This year is also going to be fabulous. It's always moving and hypnotic to see people learn a brand-new skill and to do it with open arms, and *Strictly* is a little bit of Christmas every Saturday.'

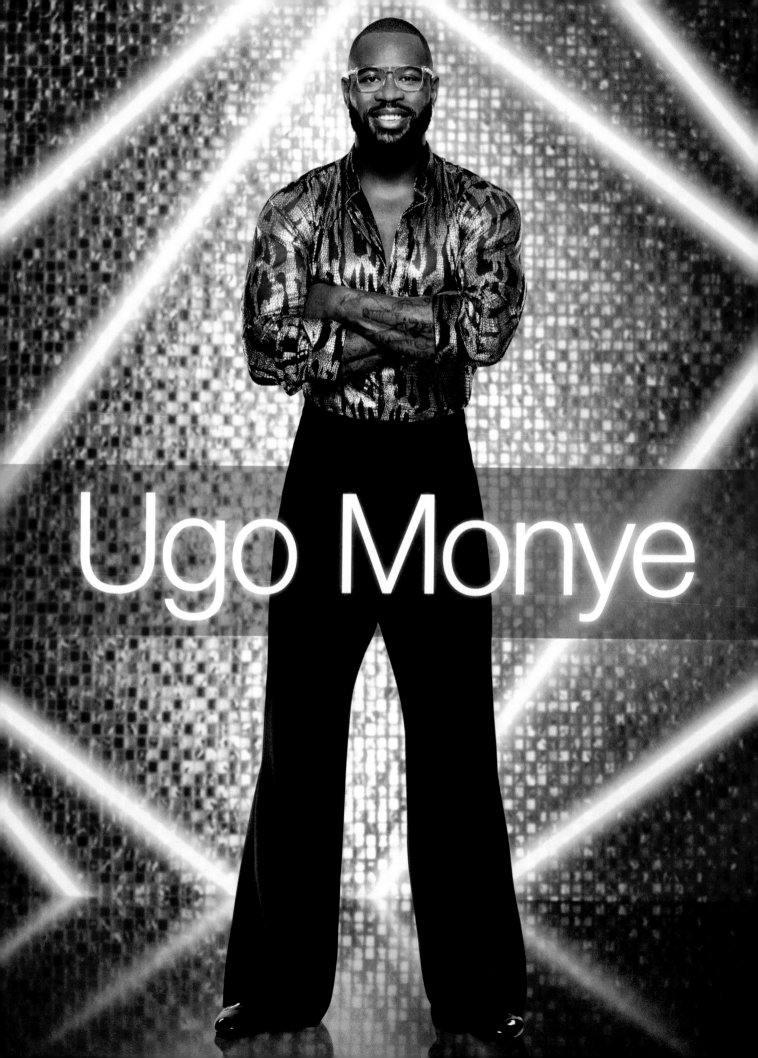

Ugo Monye

Former rugby player Ugo Monye's decision to join the *Strictly* cast was influenced by two special ladies in his life: daughters Phoenix, four, and Ruby, one.

'My daughters never got to watch me play rugby and my eldest, Phoenix, loves dancing,' he says. 'I know she will be super excited watching it, so there's a big part of me that wants to do it for them.'

In fact, Phoenix, who goes to regular ballet classes, has been trying to help Dad with a few moves.

'Phoenix has been teaching me different poses, like pliés and getting up onto tiptoes – which I currently can't do, so that's quite a humbling experience. Also, she thinks Daddy's going to be in a tutu on telly!'

While he may not be dancing in a tutu, Ugo is prepared to fully embrace the sequins and Lycra.

'I'm game for anything. If you're going to do it, you may as well go the whole hog,' he says. 'I've only seen my launch outfit, but there's plenty of sparkles and it's sheer. You only get to do it once, so I want to enjoy the experience for however long it lasts.'

Londoner Ugo signed to the Harlequins at 18 and played for England between 2008 and 2012. Since retiring from the sport in 2015, Ugo has become a popular rugby union pundit, and has also recently taken over as a team captain on the BBC's *Question of Sport*.

While Ugo, 38, is still incredibly fit, he reveals there are some aspects of his sport that are incompatible with the ballroom.

'In rugby, you are built to be stiff, robust,' he says. 'Ballroom dancing is all about poise, grace, shape and form, and that's going to be a real challenge because I'm not the most flexible of lads. So my immediate challenge is to undo everything I've learned in my rugby career.'

However, there is one advantage a life in sport has given him.

'I love to work really hard, so I'll be really diligent. I'm a better pupil now than I was at school. I like to listen, to learn, and that's going to be a big part of it. I think that self-motivation, and being competitive, will give me a good foundation.'

Although he has no formal dance experience, Ugo is a keen music lover and an enthusiastic amateur. Ugo's mum is a huge *Strictly* fan and is delighted that her son will be taking to the floor this year. She will also be a crucial part of his pre-show ritual.

'I'm bound to get nervous because I always got nervous before every rugby game I played, but I think nerves are good because it shows that you care,' he says. 'To calm me down I love listening to music. Also, I always rang my mum and said a prayer on the phone before every single match I ever played, anywhere in the world, and that won't be stopping. I'll need her support, so I'll be ringing my mum before every show.'

Ugo follows in the footsteps of many a rugby player – including series 4 runner-up Matt Dawson and series 6 quarter-finalist Austin Healey.

'Austin's already put the pressure on, telling me rugby players have generally done well so the standard has been set,' he says. 'But everyone's so excited for me and the reaction from the fans has been amazing. It's nice to know that I'm still part of that rugby family and they are all being really supportive.'

Oti Mabuse

Current champ Oti Mabuse made history last year by picking up her second consecutive glitterball, with comedian Bill Bailey. Now she's hoping to score a hat-trick with rugby star Ugo Monye.

'The great thing about sportsmen is that they know what hard work is,' she says. 'But what really matters is a person's character, and how they want to develop and grow on the show. Athletes have a different mindset, but Ugo is a presenter as well, so he's used to long studio hours, and the presenting will help him with the performance side, getting into the character of the dance.'

The new partners hit it off as soon as they met, and Oti says there will be a lot of laughter during training.

'When we first talked we spent so much time laughing, and he's got a great sense of humour,' she says. 'My first advice to him was: "There's method behind my madness, just go with it, ride the wave, because it is bumpy, but you'll absolutely love it." He's really warm and endearing and I enjoy those characteristics when I'm teaching someone. I'm really excited to get to know him and see his journey on the show.'

Oti was unveiled as Ugo's partner at the hallowed ground of Twickenham, which was a first for her.

'I've never been to a stadium in my life,' she says. 'Ugo showed me where he scored his first try for England and I could just see how proud he was. The seats were empty, but I could imagine how it feels when it's full of England supporters and you're making your country proud.'

Born in Pretoria, South Africa, Oti began dancing as a young child, following in the footsteps of her older sister, *Strictly* judge Motsi. She gained a civil engineering degree before moving to Germany to compete. Oti has a long list of titles, including eight-time South African Latin American Champion, and joined *Strictly* in 2015. Last year Oti became the first pro to retain the glitterball trophy, a year after winning with soap star Kelvin Fletcher.

'That moment was unbelievable,' she recalls. 'There are so many things going through your mind, and winning is not one of them. It's the best feeling ever because it felt like, against many odds, we did something that was not expected. I also made a lifelong friend in Bill.'

As a pupil, Oti says Bill's love of learning helped him perfect his dances.

'Bill was diligent and disciplined,' she says. 'He couldn't dance at the start, but he worked hard and every time he had the opportunity to learn, he went the extra mile. He learned about the history of the dance, the history of the steps, the character that I gave him and why he had to be that person. As a student, he went above and beyond.'

This year, Oti is delighted to see four friends – Cameron, Jowita, Nikita and Kai – joining the pro team.

'They're all amazing,' she says. 'I know Cameron from South Africa, Nikita and I trained together in Germany and I've known Kai for ten years, and they're all sweet and talented guys. I mentored Jowita on *The Greatest Dancer* and it's brilliant to see her live her dream, because she's wanted this for years. There's nothing better than seeing friends reach their goals and be happy. I'm so proud of all four of them.'

As she prepares for her eighth season in the show, the reigning champ says she has learned to expect the unexpected.

'What I love most is the element of surprise, because every year is so different for me,' she says. 'I'm looking forward to seeing what the other professionals create with their celebrities, because there's always something new there, and how the show is going to turn out. It's surreal when you're part of a live show, because everything is happening in real time and you can't predict anything.'

Dressing Room Essentials

The dressing rooms in the *Strictly Come Dancing* and *It Takes Two* studios are as individual as the judges and presenters themselves. Each one has their own personal effects around them, from the snacks that get them through Saturday filming to the music that helps them relax between filming. Now our *Strictly* stars take us behind closed doors for the first time, as they reveal the things they can't do without in their dressing rooms.

TESS DALY

My *Strictly* kit box: All those little essentials I reach for backstage during the live show. Lots of mints to keep the mouth and throat lubricated – drinking too many fluids is definitely NOT an option during a two-and-a-half-hour live show with no ad breaks! Sweets for energy when we are two hours in. Blister plasters for when the heels start to hurt. And orange highlighter pens – I'm lost without my trusty orange highlighter, which I use to highlight notes on my script; I can pick out words at 10 feet under the bright studio lights!

Framed photos of my girls, Phoebe and Amber: This will be my seventeenth year doing the show, and Phoebe will also turn 17 during this series. Hard to believe that I was pregnant with her during the very first series back in 2004.

Fridge snacks: I'm obsessed with rainbow salad snack pots and apple and peanut butter snacks to graze on. On show days there is not much time to sit down and eat a meal, so it's often just grabbing snacks on the go to keep going. Then we will usually make up for missing dinner and share a pizza at the end of the night!

My trusty 'Glam Fam': Aimee has been doing my make-up since I was in my twenties, Christian does my hair and James styles the outfits for the show. These guys truly ARE like family to me. We always have a giggle, which helps defuse any pre-show nerves. I call them my 'Good Vibe Tribe' and I love them to bits.

CRAIG REVEL HORWOOD

Snacks: A packet of crisps, a bag of peanuts, some ham and avocado – to keep hunger at bay in breaks between filming.

Diet Coke and water: To lubricate the throat for my acerbic critiques.

Two suits: One for the live show and one for the results show.

A collection of shoes: I only decide on the footwear when I know what the female judges are wearing. We like to coordinate.

Notepad: Comes with me on set to jot down my observations on the dances.

Tracksuit and trainers: In case we need to rehearse our opening dance steps or a group routine ourselves.

MOTSI MABUSE

Speakers: I like to have music on while I'm getting ready.

Fruits: Healthy snack bites I can nibble through the day.

Water: Don't forget to hydrate!

Foundation: I always have my perfect make-up foundation with me.

Make-up remover: I never leave the studio with make-up on so that's part of the process.

Lip salve: When I get nervous I chew my mouth, which is pretty hideous, so I slather this stuff on me at all times.

Twiglets: They are my life and I would say vital for any room at any time.

Toothbrush and toothpaste: For after the Twiglets …

Decaf coffee: I can't have real coffee as I wouldn't sleep for days. I love the taste, however, and nothing on earth beats a cup of instant decaf.

CLAUDIA WINKLEMAN

SHIRLEY BALLAS

A photo of my son Mark: I carry a photograph of my son in my purse anyway, so I prop him up where I can see him. He's done the show in the US and he's used to TV so I find it inspiring to see his face and if I get a little nervous I have him right there.

Tanning lotion: I will never not have tan in my room. I like to tan my feet if I've got a tea-length dress on, and I like to tan my hands and my arms.

Calm and quiet: This isn't an object, but I love peace, so no music or noise in my room.

My chicken: I have to have a whole roasted chicken because I feel like it's good luck! I started out at the beginning of the show with a chicken and every week I have one so I can pick at it throughout the day. What I don't eat during the day I take home with me.

Judi Love

As a comedian and *Loose Women* panellist, Judi Love is always up for a chat, but she'll let her feet do the talking when she takes to the *Strictly* floor. A huge fan of the show, she admits she screamed at the top of her voice when she was asked to take part.

'I was overwhelmed,' she says. 'Who wouldn't want to do *Strictly Come Dancing*? I'm so excited by the prospect of learning such a skill from a professional. The first time at the studio, seeing the signs and looking at the outfits, I couldn't believe it was really happening. So I have no idea what I'm going to be like when I actually see the dancers, the glitz and the glam and the audience.'

Born in Hackney, East London, Judi gained two degrees in social science and social work before turning her motto, 'Laughter is healing', into a new career and becoming a stand-up comedian. She joined the panel of *Loose Women* in 2020 and was a semi-finalist on *Celebrity MasterChef* the same year. The mum-of-two says her family, friends and co-stars can't wait to see her strut her stuff.

'My *Loose Women* girls have just been very supportive, telling me to fully embrace it, have fun,' she says. 'Everybody I know who's already had the Strictly experience says the same thing: "It's hard work, but you're going to enjoy it. It's a life-changer."

'My family reacted with utter disbelief that I am going to be dancing live in front of millions of viewers, but they're really excited and supportive. I think when they actually see me dressed up and ready to dance it's going to be a very emotional moment.'

Judi's daughter and son will also be cheering her on.

'My children are my biggest supporters, and all the mums at their schools will be cheering for me. They're very excited.'

Judi is keen to throw herself headlong at the sequins and sparkles – although she says dancing in heels may be her biggest challenge.

'I'm ready to be *Strictly*-fied. I'm looking forward to the wigs, the eyelashes, the outfits, the shoes – and I want to see how glam they can go. The way they make the dresses is so bespoke and flattering, and I'm excited to see if I feel different in those glamorous clothes.

'I'm always in sliders, so I'm a bit nervous about the heels. I'm one of those women who can't even walk in heels. I can dance in them on a Friday night with my girls, but in a professional capacity, I'm not so sure.'

While Judi loves to hit the dance floor on a night out, she has no formal dance training and says Latin might come more naturally to her than ballroom.

'I'm good at finding a rhythm,' she says. 'I've got the Caribbean mum dance down – as long as I can find a beat I'm good, so the Salsa and Cha-cha-cha would probably suit me best. But the Waltz and Tango are so out of my comfort zone. I've never danced with a straight back in my life, or in hold, and they require so much concentration and precise movement; thinking from toe to head and knowing exactly where your feet are going. That will be hard for me.'

Not usually one to hold back on her opinions, Judi insists she's ready to face the *Strictly* judges and take their comments on the chin.

'No one likes being judged, but these guys are professionals. They've trained and studied and put their bodies through a lot of hard work to gain their phenomenal skill. They're talking to me about something that I'm not skilled in, so who am I not to be happy? I have to learn from constructive criticism and try to do better.'

Graziano Di Prima

Sicilian dancer Graziano Di Prima may be teamed with *Loose Women* star Judi Love, but he's planning to keep her on a tight schedule.

'I'm having the best time ever,' he says. 'We are going to laugh a lot, but she wants to work hard and to do her best, which I'm really happy about. When we were paired I said, "Are you ready to train with me for eight to ten hours a day?" She said, "Are you kidding me? Ten hours?" But she really wants to learn to dance, so she is willing to put the hours in.

'We want to have a great season and a great journey, in an enjoyable way. So I'll find a way to train for a few hours, then give her a break, laugh a bit, and then back to the training! We're going to have a brilliant time.'

For the pairing, Graziano met comedian Judi at the iconic Hackney Empire, where he was hiding behind the stage curtain.

'When the curtain went up, I said, "Ciao, bella," and Judi was screaming so loud, we had to repeat it four times, because she drowned out my voice,' he laughs. 'Then I came off stage, we hugged and we were both so happy. She told me she couldn't wait to dance with me and we hit it off straight away. She is such a huge personality and I asked her to be herself, because I want to bring her as a person into the dance. I want to put her sassiness onto the *Strictly* dance floor.'

In their first moments together, Graziano showed his new partner a few steps and was delighted with the result.

'I tried Judi out in a basic ballroom hold, and she's got a brilliant frame,' he says. 'We also did two steps of Salsa and she picked up the steps very quickly, with a lot of laughter along the way. Now I just have to find out how she copes with her routines, in a practical way.'

Born in Sicily, Graziano began dancing at the age of six and moved to Bologna at 17 to train and compete. He went on to become Italian Latin Champion and has also represented Belgium at the World Championships. He joined *Strictly* in 2018, dancing with DJ Vick Hope. Graziano holds the Guinness World Record for the most Botafogo dance steps in 30 seconds, with a total of 90, achieved on *It Takes Two*.

Now an established part of the *Strictly* family, Graziano has been impressed with new recruits Kai, Jowita, Cameron and Nikita during the group dance rehearsals.

'Their introduction to *Strictly* was three weeks of group rehearsal and filming, which is full on,' he says. 'With 17 other dancers, you need to be aware of what is going on around you and that's not something that you do every day because, as a professional dancer, it's usually yourself and your partner. You don't usually dance with so many others beside you, passing, doing lifts and twirls, so it's been interesting to see new people coming in and doing so well. All the pros have made sure they are comfortable and happy, and it's been beautiful. They're amazing.'

Graziano is excited to get into the training room and get dancing.

'I'm looking forward to having fun with Judi,' he says. 'I could feel our chemistry from the first moment, and that's something you either have or you don't. I think she will be quite a surprise on the series. I can't wait.'

With pro and celeb interviews, backstage gossip and tons of fun, *Strictly Come Dancing: It Takes Two* is back with a bang – and host Rylan is waltzing into the studio with a spring in his step.

'I can't wait to meet this year's celebs, but I always look forward to seeing the amazing new pro dancers, as well as the returning pros and our fantastic crew,' he says. 'I genuinely miss them when we're not filming. I'm so excited about being back with the gang and getting stuck into the performances and all the gossip as usual. It's like returning to school and seeing all your friends again after a long break.'

This year, Rylan will be sharing presenting duties with new co-host Janette Manrara – already a much-loved part of the *Strictly* family. The former pro, who reached the Final with HRVY in series 18, has always been a regular on the *It Takes Two* sofa and she and Rylan already get on like a house on fire.

'I ADORE Janette,' he says. 'She is an absolute pocket rocket and I look forward to her becoming my new TV wife – although I'm six foot four inches and she's around one foot eight inches, so I can't wait to see how that turns out!'

The presenter has been picking up some moves since joining *It Takes Two* in 2019 and is hoping to impress Janette with his fancy footwork. 'The *It Takes Two* team definitely put me through my paces each year, but now, having a pro dancer as a co-presenter, I'd better dust my dancing shoes off,' he says. 'I'll Cha-Cha-Chat my way through it.'

His new co-star also featured in his favourite dance of last year.

'I really loved Janette and HRVY when they danced to Harry Styles's "Golden",' he says. 'I just thought it was a really beautiful dance and it made me adore the track.'

A lifelong fan of *Strictly* himself, Rylan is looking forward to seeing the contestants take to the floor for the first time – and he'll be looking out for potential finalists among the novices.

'I always love week 1,' he says. 'It's anyone's game and it's really a great show, because you get to see everyone perform for the first time. That's when it's cemented that we're in for a great series and the level of excitement begins to rise. At the start, you never know who is going to be a fantastic dancer and sometimes, to get there, they go on a journey, so I can't wait to see them all perform and work their magic. This year, as always, the line-up is great. This bunch is so varied – it's very exciting.

'I think Tilly Ramsay may take to the floor really well as I know she loves to dance. I'm sure dad Gordon is putting the pressure on! I also think Judi Love will be a great watch and entertaining on the dance floor – I bet she loves a glitter dress. They all look amazing, so bring it on!'

Rylan says his work on *Strictly* tops the agenda when it comes to friends, family and fans he meets on the street. 'Everyone loves *Strictly* – it's all people want to talk about when the show is on,' he laughs. 'It's mainly, "Can you get me tickets?" – I have a long waiting list!'

As he heads to the studio for his third year on the sister show, Rylan is staying tight-lipped about any upcoming changes but says there are bound to be some fun new additions to the regular features. 'As always, our production team are absolute superstars and I'm sure they'll have some tricks up their sleeve!'

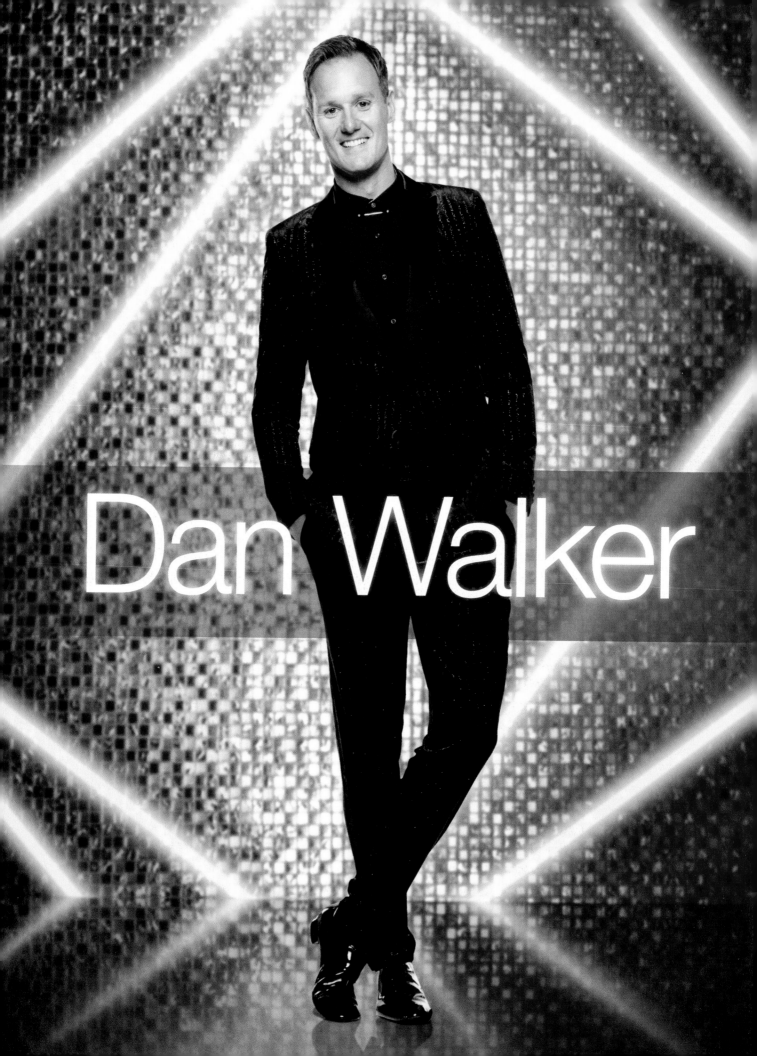
Dan Walker

Swapping the sofa for the Samba, Dan Walker is following in the footsteps of many a *BBC Breakfast* colleague, including two former champs in Ore Oduba and Chris Hollins.

'A lot of my colleagues have taken part over the years, including Naga Munchetty, Carol Kirkwood and Mike Bushell, and they have all really enjoyed it. They've been lovely with their advice and are fully supportive – so hopefully I won't let the *Breakfast* team down.'

Family man Dan has quite a team cheering him on at home as well, as wife Sarah and his three kids were behind his decision to sign up.

'My children sat me down at Christmas and said, "Dad, this year, if you're offered *Strictly*, will you please do it?"' he says. 'I've got two daughters, who are 14 and 12 and very much into dancing, and as anyone who's got kids of that age will know, it's rare to do something that they are fully invested in. So they're all excited.

'Also, after years of reading headlines about awful stuff, I just wanted to have a giggle and learn a new skill. There aren't many opportunities where you get to learn from people who are literally the best on the planet. So I might be terrible, but at least I'll be learning from someone who is excellent.'

Born and raised in Crawley, Sussex, Dan began his broadcasting career at Sheffield's Hallam FM after winning a competition for young sports commentators. He went on to become an award-winning sports reporter on both radio and TV, presenting the BBC's *Football Focus* and Radio 5 Live's *Afternoon Edition*. He joined the BBC *Breakfast* team in 2016.

During his *Strictly* stint, Dan will be juggling his day job with training, but he's confident he can still handle the early starts.

'I've always been busy,' he says. 'I don't quite know how it's going to work with 3 a.m. starts, but I'll put the training in where I can. I'm determined that I won't go out of the competition for not trying hard enough. Talent might be my curse, but I will definitely do as much training as I possibly can.'

At 6 foot 6 inches, Dan is the tallest of the celebrities and he says his partner might have trouble reining in his long arms.

'My pro partner will need to be very patient and have quick reflexes to avoid the elbows, because I can flail a little bit and I need space on the dance floor,' he says. 'I'm a good student and I love working with other people. But probably the number-one priority for me is to have a partner who likes a giggle and can laugh along with my foolishness.'

To prepare for the show, 44-year-old Dan has been watching online videos and taking tips from his oldest daughter, who attends dance classes.

'She's shown me a few moves but has also started shaking her head in despair when we have a kitchen disco every now and again,' he laughs. 'My ten-year-old son is a proper little mover as well. They're really excited. Normally what happens is some music comes on, I move like a goon and they say, "Don't do that on the telly, Dad!"'

As a sports fan, Dan is taking the contest seriously – but he's aware there's some tough competition.

'I am very competitive about everything,' he says. 'But I think my competitiveness is balanced out by my understanding of my limitations. I'm not going to allow my desire to do well outstrip my own ability; I'm just going to have a bit of fun and enjoy myself!

'I just want to learn as much as I can, meet some amazing people – which has already happened – and enjoy the experience of being on the biggest show on British TV, which is not an opportunity you get very often.'

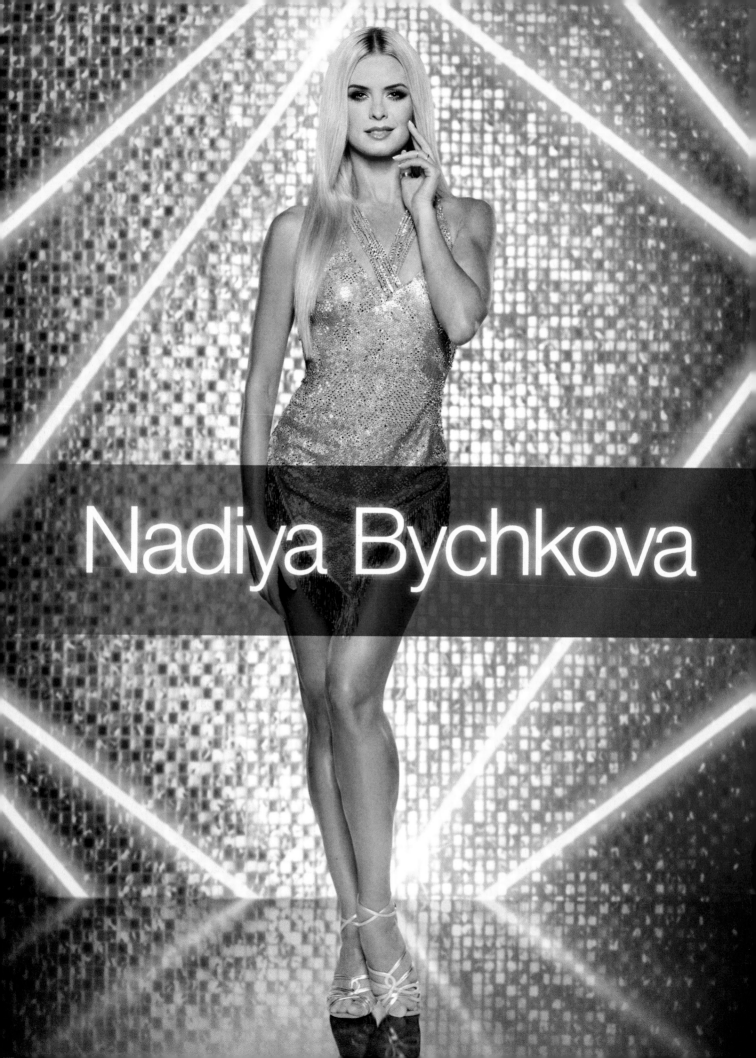

Nadiya Bychkova

With around 500 outfits to create per series, Head Designer Vicky Gill and her team work tirelessly to make every single one fabulous.

It's not just the final look that the costume team are considering, but the impact on the environment and what will happen to each outfit after the show. The team have a three-pronged attack to ensure that each of the costumes has a maximum number of wears, whether it is on the *Strictly* set or elsewhere, with some ending up at dancewear company DSI, where they can be hired by competitive dancers and other production companies, some being recycled for the show and others donated to good causes.

'Everything gets used at some point – nothing's a throw-away,' says Vicky. 'Some garments are designed with a hire scheme in mind, so, while it's perfect for a dance on *Strictly*, it can also be hired and reused around the world, within the *Dancing with the Stars* family. Others go to DSI because they fit perfectly within the competitive ballroom and Latin world, so they get to live another life on the dance floor. Sometimes people hire them for different productions that have nothing to do with *Strictly*, but the outfit just fits the bill.'

As well as the showrooms and storage at DSI, *Strictly* has its own storeroom at Elstree and Vicky keeps many garments in her own studio. While you'll never see the exact same outfit on the *Strictly* floor twice, many of the looks hold an element of past glories.

'We have to be creative with our thinking,' explains Vicky. 'The dress itself will not come back in its entirety, but it may be the base, it may be the outer layer or part of the skirt that is added to a new look. But all elements will be used in one way or another, and nothing gets wasted.

'Often, it's time pressure that determines how we repurpose and recreate garments, because if something's not working and we only have two hours before a show, we look at what we have to hand and see how we can make it work with the lighting and the set so that everybody is happy.'

If a dress is too recognisable or has been in *Strictly* storage for a couple of years, it might be donated to a theatre school or an amateur group for use in their productions.

'We're helping the planet by remaking and reusing, but storage also has implications for the environment, so rather than enlarging storage space, we will give outfits away,' says Vicky.

In the men's department, getting the maximum wear is a little more straightforward. 'With tailoring, we don't want it to be a one-hit wonder, we want longevity,' explains Vicky. 'The pro boys will have dinner suits that will last them a few seasons, if not longer, and we try to build on that by introducing different designs. So a piece from the main show may move across into a group dance number, or it'll go on the live tour. They certainly live a life by the end of the run.'

An essential jacket, for example, will get a minimum of 30 wears, and that figure doubles if it is worn every day on the live tour.

'With men's jackets and suits, we change them by styling them with different pieces, so it might be different shirt colours, or changing the combination of jacket and trousers,' says Vicky. 'We try not to embellish classic pieces too much, unless it's something understated, because more bling makes it harder to utilise the jacket on other occasions. If we do want to add sparkle, we add the embellishment to a fine mesh, which we can hand-sew onto the jacket so that it can be easily removed after the performance.'

The most frequently used items on set are the shoes, as much for comfort as for environmental reasons. Celebrities will have dance shoes that they use throughout the series, but the pro shoes can last for season after season.

'We have hundreds of shoes stored in shoe boxes,' says Vicky. 'If it's a shoe that's only worn once, they'll definitely wear it again in the following season. They become very comfortable after a few wears, so they don't want brand-new shoes all the time. They will wear them until the heel goes or they're not fit for purpose.'

Overall, Vicky estimates that a third of the dresses you see are made new, a third are re-styled or made from repurposed material and a third come from the *Strictly* stockroom. Whatever the origin of the outfit, viewers can rest assured it will go on to have a fabulous life after its starring role in *Strictly*.

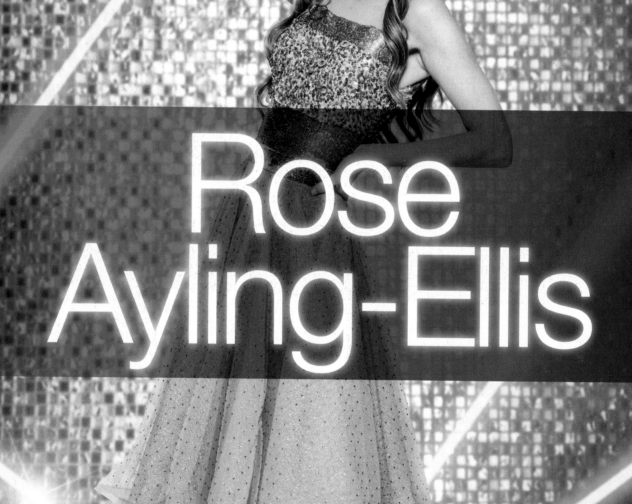

Rose Ayling-Ellis

EastEnders actress Rose Ayling-Ellis has already made soap history by becoming Albert Square's first deaf resident played by a deaf actress. Now, she's blazing a trail on the *Strictly* dance floor.

'As the first deaf person in *Strictly*, I want to break the stereotype around what deaf people can or can't do,' she says. 'A lot of people think we can't enjoy music and enjoy dancing, and this is a good platform to challenge that stereotype.'

Rose says her phone has been pinging with supportive messages since she was announced in the line-up, and the reaction from the deaf community has been overwhelming.

'I have been really lucky that everyone has been super-supportive and my deaf friends in particular are so excited for me,' she says. 'It will also be interesting to see the reaction from a hearing audience. I hope it will bring a lot of positives and change people's attitudes, which will help deaf people have better experiences and perhaps encourage more people to get involved in the industry.'

Rose got the acting bug as a child after meeting film director Ted Evans at an event held by the National Deaf Children's Society. He cast her in his award-winning film *The End*, and she went on to join the Deafinitely Youth Theatre as well as starring in several stage productions, including *Faith, Hope and Charity* at the National Theatre. She has played Frankie Lewis in *EastEnders* since 2020.

Rose's acting skills will come in handy in the more dramatic dances, and she says she'll be creating a character for the sassier routines.

'The dance I'm most keen to do is the Tango because it's very different to who I am,' she says.

'It's a very intense, sexy dance and that's not me – I'm normally very polite. I don't do sexy. I think it will be a challenge for me, so I'll need to create a character to put me in the right frame of mind. The Jive is the one that I'm most nervous of, because it's so fast and there's a lot of jumping and kicking. It's non-stop and there's hardly time to catch your breath.'

To prepare for the show, the 26-year-old actress has been working out and improving her fitness.

'I tried to join the gym, but that wasn't very successful, so I started to exercise with my friends,' she says. 'I do hot yoga so I can stretch, and I recently started doing weights to try to get strength in my arms, because I've got no muscle in my arms. I can now manage a 61kg weight in a dead lift.'

She's also been trying on her dancing shoes, and it seems they may take some getting used to.

'The two things I'm worried about are tripping over in the live show and wearing the heels,' she explains. 'I can walk okay in heels, but dancing shoes are different, so I feel like that could be a challenge. But *Strictly* is a great opportunity to just go for it, get the full glitter, tan, hair, and get glammed up. And I've never had a spray tan, so I am looking forward to that.'

Rose's only dance experience is ballet as a child and some classes in theatre training, but she says her years as an actor have prepared her for the judges' comments.

'I went to art college and I'm in acting, so I see constructive criticism as a big part of improving yourself,' she says. 'Criticism is the only way that you can get better, because if no one says what's wrong, how can you improve?'

While she's keen to lift the glitterball, Rose is also rooting for all the other couples on the floor.

'Everyone is so lovely, I don't think I can see them as competition,' she says. 'I want everyone to be great and dance well, and then it'll be bigger competition for me. In terms of my own chances, I'm just going to do my best, take one day at a time, one routine at a time, and see how it goes.'

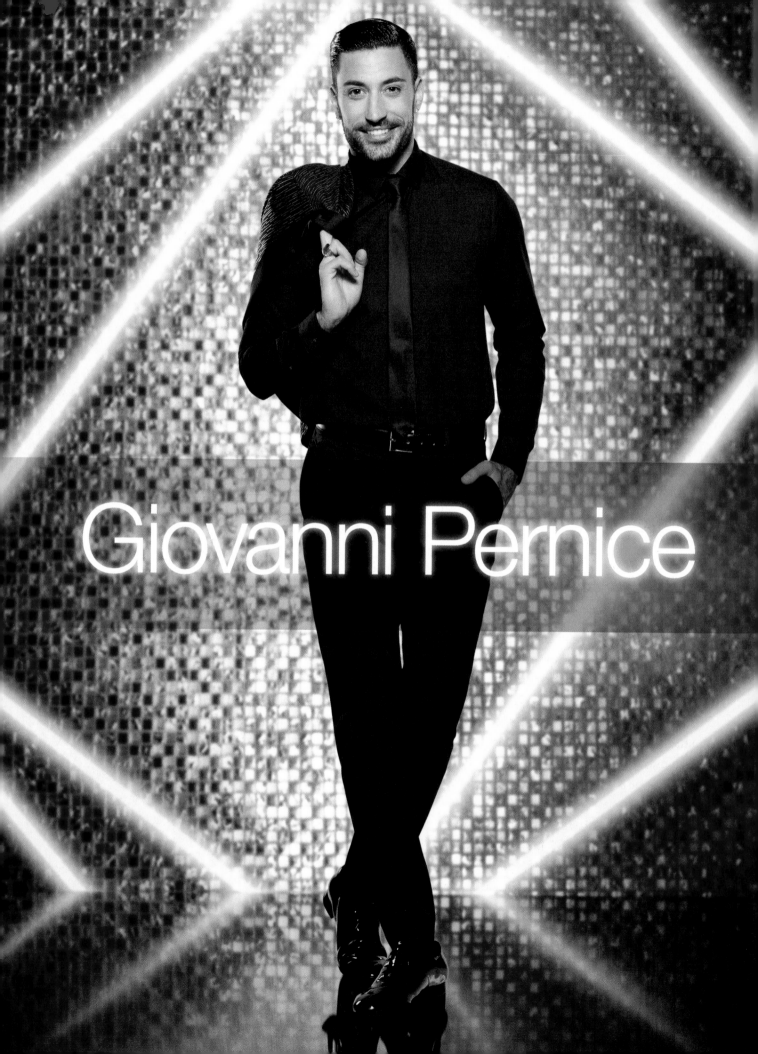

Giovanni Pernice

Italian pro Giovanni Pernice has already reached the Final three times and is hoping it will be fourth time lucky with actress Rose Ayling-Ellis. As befitting an *EastEnders* star, Rose was first introduced to her new dance partner in Albert Square.

'We met in the real Albert Square, which I didn't know existed,' says Giovanni. 'I thought it was just a set for *EastEnders*, but there is a place in London and it was lovely. I walked into this beautiful garden and saw Rose and I was very happy that she was going to be my celebrity partner. She's a lovely young lady. Obviously, Rose was happy, too!'

As he is partnering Rose, *Strictly*'s first deaf contestant, Giovanni is taking a slightly different approach to the rehearsal process but says the fundamentals of teaching the dance stay the same.

'Obviously there will be some things that will be a little different, but Rose is really keen and really wants to learn, so I think she will be a great student,' he says. 'In all the choreography I'm going to do I'll make sure that she can follow my body language. She may need to learn more by muscle memory than through the music, so it will be a different approach, but we will figure it out and I'm sure we will work brilliantly together. I have also learned some sign language – the basics – but I am planning to learn a lot more along the way.'

Still in the early stages, Giovanni is looking forward to finding out Rose's strengths in the rehearsal room, but he believes she may be an all-rounder.

'I think she will be good at Latin and ballroom,' he says. 'With every single celebrity you need to spend time with them in the room to see what they are good at, but I have a feeling she will be good at everything. I have told her it's going be a lot of work, but we'll make sure that both of us enjoy the process. Realistically, that is the key. You have to enjoy it and then everything else comes together.'

The Sicilian left home at 14 to study dance in Bologna and began competing as an adult in 2008. Four years later, he was crowned Italian Champion. He has also competed in numerous international dance competitions all over the world. He joined *Strictly* in 2015, reaching the Final with *Coronation Street* star Georgia May Foote and scoring a perfect 40 for their incredible Charleston. He has been a finalist twice since, in 2017 with Debbie McGee and the following year with Faye Tozer. Last year he made it to the Semi-final with *Good Morning Britain* presenter Ranvir Singh.

'Ranvir was a brilliant student and really wanted to learn how to dance,' he says. 'She's a mum and was doing *GMB* in the morning, so it was a lot to juggle, but she really committed. She really improved a lot, and that's what you want to see as a teacher. It's all about that.'

As the new series kicks off, Giovanni is thrilled to be back in the studio and dancing once again.

'I have loved being back in the group rehearsals and it's been amazing for us all to be together, doing what we love to do, which is dancing,' he says. 'At the end of the day, *Strictly Come Dancing* is the best show on television and we're dancers, so I have the best job I could ask for. I am just so excited to start.'

Strictly Word Search

V	S	H	E	E	D	L	Z	J	A	B	B	X	U	C
Y	E	L	R	I	H	S	T	R	U	M	B	A	S	S
L	P	N	O	M	T	Q	A	R	C	G	A	R	C	F
E	F	C	O	O	R	B	J	I	V	E	Z	X	L	T
C	F	O	L	L	A	B	P	X	I	L	B	E	A	S
H	E	U	F	K	C	A	R	N	E	W	R	S	D	H
A	D	R	E	W	O	T	P	V	N	E	T	U	O	O
R	A	T	C	X	T	W	E	B	N	R	H	B	F	W
L	E	A	N	C	O	R	R	L	E	O	T	A	R	D
E	X	B	A	O	G	Q	U	E	S	R	O	M	T	A
S	F	Z	D	I	N	D	N	F	E	L	I	B	S	N
T	Z	T	A	S	A	L	S	A	K	F	N	P	A	C
O	C	R	O	U	T	R	L	O	X	Y	E	L	A	E
N	C	E	L	Y	E	L	I	A	B	L	L	I	B	H
T	R	I	P	P	R	C	N	E	I	V	L	I	R	F

Hidden in the grid are 15 words connected to *Strictly Come Dancing*, with clues below. Remember, they can go forwards and backwards, up and down, and diagonally. How many can you spot?

★ *Strictly* judge Mr Horwood (5, 5)

★ Argentine dance (5)

★ Fast twirling Waltz (8)

★ American swing dance (4)

★ Head judge Ms Ballas (7)

★ Stretchy one-piece worn by dancers (7)

★ Centre stage of the ballroom, where the couples perform (5, 5)

★ Series 18 winner (4, 6)

★ The dance of love (5)

★ Surname of Motsi and Oti (6)

★ Dance popular in the 1920s and introduced to *Strictly* in series 7 (10)

★ Freestyle dance only finalists get to perform (9)

★ Blackpool ----- Ballroom hosts *Strictly* once a year (5)

★ Latin party dance with lots of armography (5)

★ Black-tie event with dancing (4)

Strictly Crossword

Sparkly pens at the ready! It's time to test your *Strictly* knowledge with our fun crossword.

See page 127 for answers.

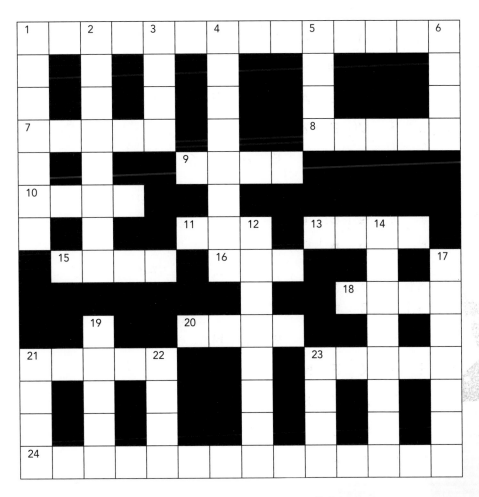

Across

1. *It Takes Two* presenter (5, 5, 4)
7. Presenters, like Claudia and Tess (5)
8. Brazilian party dance (5)
9. Blue star Lee, series 16 contestant (4)
10. *Strictly*'s live band can certainly raise the – – – – (4)
11. Mr Chambers, series 6 winner (3)
13. Dave – – – –, *Strictly*'s band leader (4)
15. Quick or slow, a movement in dance (4)
16. 'Single Ladies (– – – a Ring on It)' – Beyoncé song Catherine Tyldesley danced to in series 17 (3)
18. – – – – style – a dance without rules, like the showdance (4)
20. To twirl round (4)
21. Latin dance of love (5)
23. Mr Jackson, series 3 finalist (5)
24. South African professional who was partnered with Caroline Quentin in series 18 (8, 6)

Down

1. First name of the Rev. Coles, series 15 contestant (7)
2. Classic Cole Porter song Ann Widdecombe and Anton Du Beke danced a Charleston to (4, 2, 2)
3. Front page – – – –, like *Strictly*'s new series (4)
4. American swing dance, originating in the 1920s (5, 3)
5. Prince song Kate Silverton danced a Cha-cha-cha to in series 16 (4)
6. Ms Mushtuk, *Strictly* professional (4)
12. All-singing, all-dancing stage shows behind one of *Strictly*'s themed weeks (8)
14. First name of actor Quentin, series 18 contestant (8)
17. Surname of Italian pro Giovanni (7)
19. Surname of series 18 contestants Jacqui and Maisie (5)
21. First name of doctor who competed in series 16 (4)
22. – – – – Dedicoat, the voice of *Strictly* (4)
23. Chris Hollins's 'team' name with Ola Jordan (4)

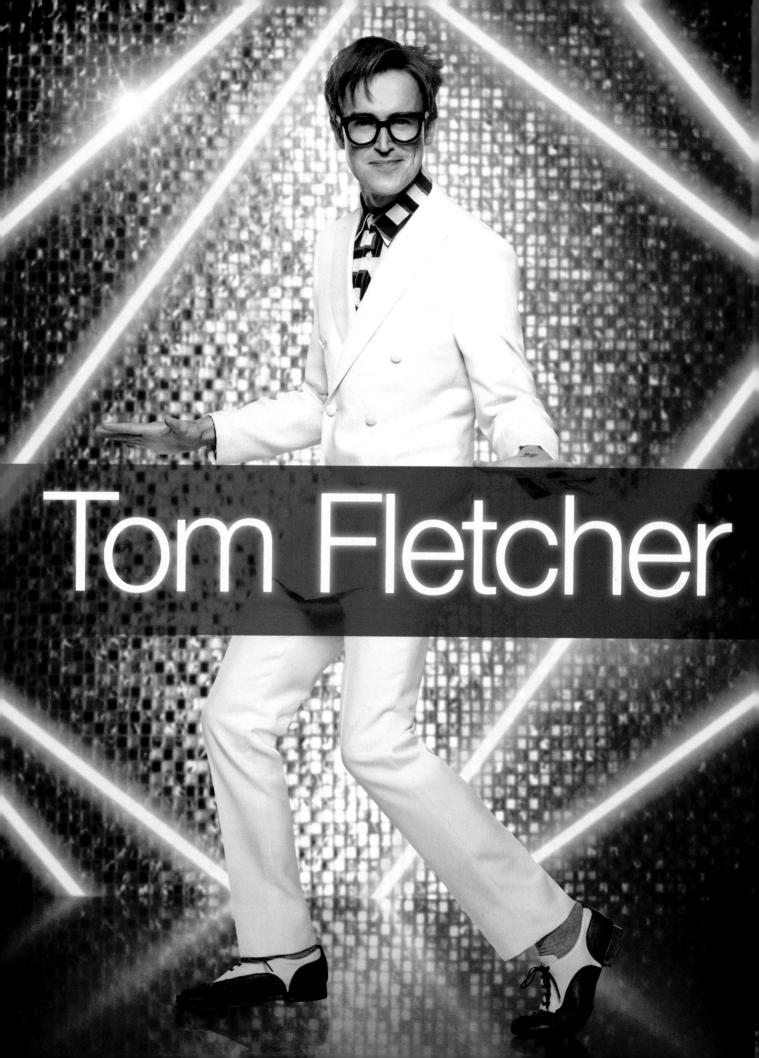

Tom Fletcher

Musician and author Tom Fletcher is following in the footsteps of bandmate Harry Judd, who danced his way to *Strictly* victory in 2011, and he admits they are big shoes to fill.

'Secretly, I've wanted to do *Strictly* since Harry won because I watched him every week in the studio,' he says. 'It's been part of McFly's history because it was an amazing time for our band, but *Strictly* was his thing. Now, after ten years, I feel the time is right.

'Because he won it, there is a bit of pressure for me to go far, but I just want to have a fun experience. You only get to do *Strictly* once – the show is a national treasure – so I want to have the best time and not worry about competing with Harry Judd!'

Drummer Harry was the first person Tom talked to about joining the 2021 cast, and he soon got the seal of approval.

'I wanted to make sure he was happy with me taking part, but he was fully supportive and said that I should totally do it and I would have the best time,' he said. 'I haven't been able to stop Harry talking about *Strictly* for ten years, but I don't know whether I should trust his advice or if he's secretly steering me in the wrong direction, because he's quite competitive. I don't know how far he wants me to get.'

In 2004, Tom formed four-piece band McFly with songwriting partner Danny Jones, Dougie Poynter and Harry, and they became the youngest band ever to reach number one with their debut album. As well as contributing to his own band's success, Tom has written or co-written hits for Busted, One Direction and 5 Seconds of Summer.

Now a dad of three, Tom says his oldest son, Buzz, now seven, was also behind his decision to try on the dancing shoes.

'Over the last couple of years, Buzz has been such a huge fan of *Strictly* and is really emotionally invested. He cried when Chris Ramsey was voted off a couple of years ago and he really gets into it. So when they asked if I would do it, I thought he would love that, so I had to say yes.

'Buzz is really looking forward to Movie Week and Musicals Week, so I hope I get that far. He gives me loads of ideas of what he wants me to dance to, based on whatever movies he's into at the time, which is really sweet.'

Tom's dance experience includes a little tap training at theatre school and dancing on stage with the band, but he believes the *Strictly* experience will be very different.

'I'm used to performing live, but onstage I've got my three bandmates, I've got a guitar and a mic stand in front of me, and they're like my shield or safety blanket,' he says. 'Taking the guitar away, even at a McFly show for a few minutes, feels weird, so suddenly being on my own on the dance floor, without my bandmates and with no instrument, is going to be scary. But it will be fun, too.'

Tom, 36, says he seized the opportunity to take to the floor now 'while I'm still, like, relatively youthful and able to jump around'.

'When Harry did it, he had ten years on me and he was in much better shape than me then, as he is now,' he says. 'I can't even touch my toes. I'm so not flexible. When I signed up for *Strictly*, I vowed to get in shape, do yoga and Pilates, and eat well, but that soon went out of the window. I think I'm in for a shock when we start actually dancing, but by the time I leave *Strictly* I'd like to be able to touch my toes!'

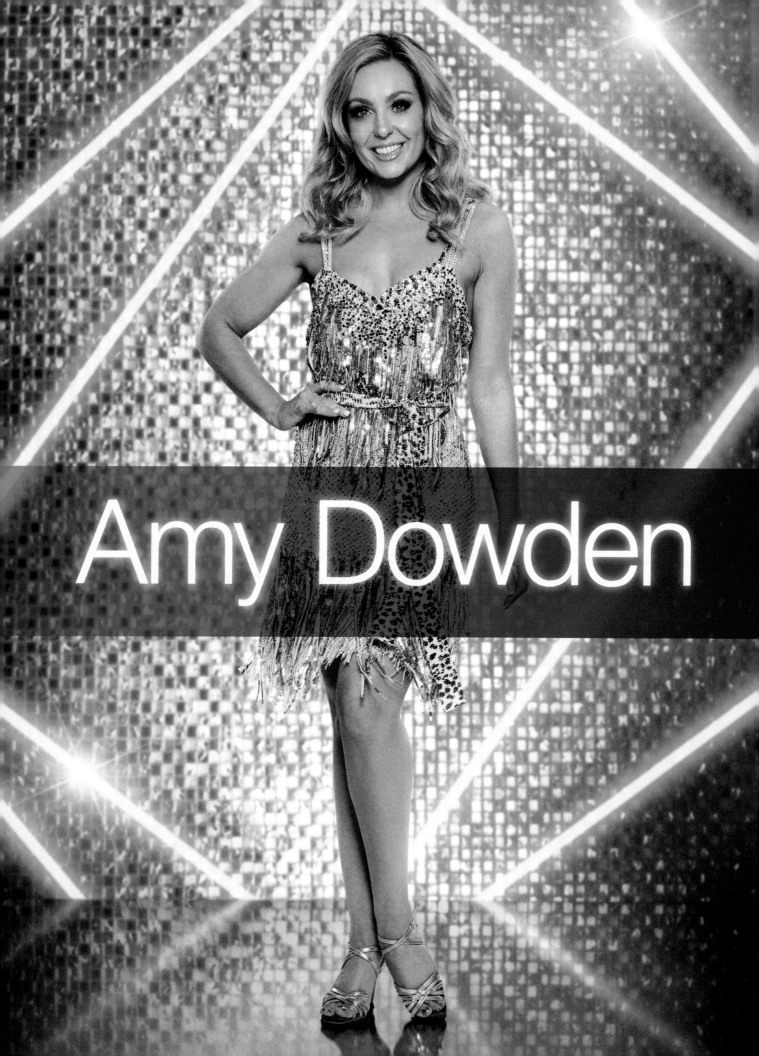

Amy Dowden

As a huge McFly fan, Amy Dowden was over the moon to be partnered with guitarist Tom Fletcher, and she was in for a huge surprise when the pairing was revealed on the launch show.

'For the first meeting, I turned up to the McFly HQ and the whole band was there, waiting to sing for me,' she says. 'I got my own private McFly performance and I couldn't believe it.

'I am absolutely thrilled, honoured and super excited to be dancing with Tom. We've only known each other a couple of days and we already get on really well. He has the same values as me, he's a real family man and works really hard. We are so alike, it's unreal.'

The group's drummer is former Strictly champ Harry Judd, and Amy says he is buzzing for his bandmate's time on the show.

'Harry had the most incredible time on Strictly,' she says. 'He hasn't taught Tom any dancing, but I know they've been talking endlessly about sequins, spray tans – you name it. All his bandmates want to come and support him from the sidelines, but I don't think we'll be able to keep Harry away!'

The Welsh dancer and choreographer says her new pupil's early dance moves show some promise.

'I'm impressed so far,' she says. 'Tom needs to work on the hip action, but, as a musician, he has an abundance of musicality, and that helps with picking up the timing for the steps. Plus, he's got a great work ethic, so it's my job to teach him dancing and get the best out of him.

'At the moment, he's a little more ballroom because he's got really good posture, but I do think there's a Latin dancer in there, too. I thought, after playing the guitar for so long, he'd have quite rounded shoulders, but he has a lovely top line, which is great for ballroom.'

While Amy has her eye on the prize, she is also aiming to please some very special Strictly viewers.

'I know Tom's three little boys are so excited to watch him dance, and I know his eldest, Buzz, is a huge Strictly fan, so I really want to make his family happy,' she says. 'I'd love to get to the Final, but we'll take every week at a time. My job is to get the best I possibly can out of Tom and, most importantly, for him to enjoy the Strictly experience and to fall in love with dancing.'

Born and raised in Caerphilly, Amy began dancing at the age of eight and is a four-time British National Finalist and a British National Champion, making her one of the highest-ranking ballroom and Latin dancers in the UK. Amy joined Strictly in 2017 and reached the Final with CBBC presenter Karim Zeroual two years later. In series 18, she danced with Afghanistan veteran and TV star JJ Chalmers.

'I enjoyed every second of my time with JJ,' she says. 'He was the perfect student. He worked so hard.

'With JJ, there were certain things his body couldn't do because of his injuries, but he never said, "I can't do that." It was more, "Let's find a way." He ended up doing things that his body shouldn't have been able to do and he said that Strictly was the best rehab he could have asked for. I was so proud of each and every number and how hard he worked. I admire his dedication, his motivation and the way he approaches things. He really is an inspiring man.'

A lifelong Strictly devotee herself, Amy can't wait to be back on that hallowed dance floor.

'I live and breathe Strictly,' she says. 'I don't think I could possibly love it any more! I can't wait to be beside Tom on his Strictly journey, to watch him improve, hopefully, week by week, and I really hope to make Tom's family proud.'

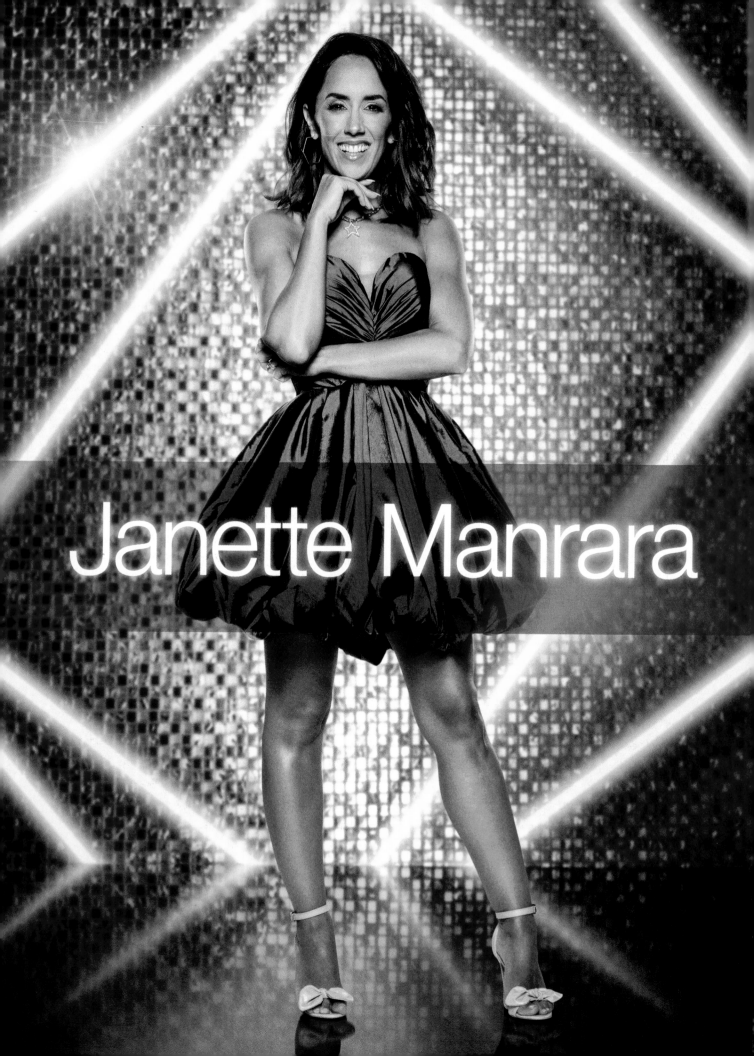

Janette Manrara

After eight years of strutting her stuff on the dance floor, Janette Manrara is taking on a new challenge – as the presenter of *It Takes Two*.

The *Strictly* pro is taking over hosting duties from Zoe Ball for two days a week, sharing the spin-off show with Rylan. It's a dream come true for Janette, even though it means hanging up her *Strictly* dance shoes.

'When I met Zoe Ball on the *It Takes Two* couch for the first time in 2013, she was the kindest, loveliest person and she was so interested in dancing and in all the couples,' she says. 'I remember leaving that first day thinking, "That would be the dream job for me someday – to sit and talk about dancing." Now my dream has come true and that's incredible.

'When the opportunity arose, it was the easiest "yes" but the hardest goodbye, because it meant I wouldn't be dancing on *Strictly*. But I'm so excited and thrilled that they trust me to take over the show with Rylan. I just want to make Zoe and all the *Strictly* fans proud.'

Janette's dance experience and close bond with her fellow pros means she is the perfect choice for the couples' chats on the *It Takes Two* couch, and she'll get to see plenty of her former colleagues during their weekly catch-ups.

'I've always loved hearing about everybody's journey and supporting each couple whenever I can so in that way not much will change. I'll still be there to offer encouragement, but now I'll be giving that support from the *It Takes Two* sofa.'

Although she will be sorely missed by her *Strictly* pro dancer colleagues, Janette will be cheering them on every Saturday night.

'For me the pros are the roots of how incredible *Strictly Come Dancing* is, coming up with the great routines and teaching the celebrities to achieve the amazing things they do, while the celebrities work so hard and really challenge themselves. So I'm looking forward to championing both the pros and the celebrities and giving each of the couples a kind ear to listen each week.'

Having reached the Final with HRVY in 2020, Janette is going out on a high – but she has enjoyed every single series since she first took to the floor, dancing with Julien Macdonald, in 2013.

'I've had an incredible eight years, and every one of my celebrities is still a really great friend. I ended with a bang with HRVY. To finally get to the Final was a dream come true.

'But there have been so many highlights. The Salsa with Jake Wood in my second year. The Trolls dance with Aston Merrygold was iconic – I never thought I would be dancing the Cha-cha-cha dressed as a troll. The Contemporary dance with Paralympic champion Will Bayley was so emotional. Will has such an inspirational story, so to be able to share it through dance was incredible. It was the first time that I cried after I performed with anyone on *Strictly*. Most recently, dancing to "One" from *A Chorus Line* with HRVY in the Final was very special. It was my last dance on *Strictly* and one of my favourite dances ever, so I'm going to hold that really close to my heart forever.'

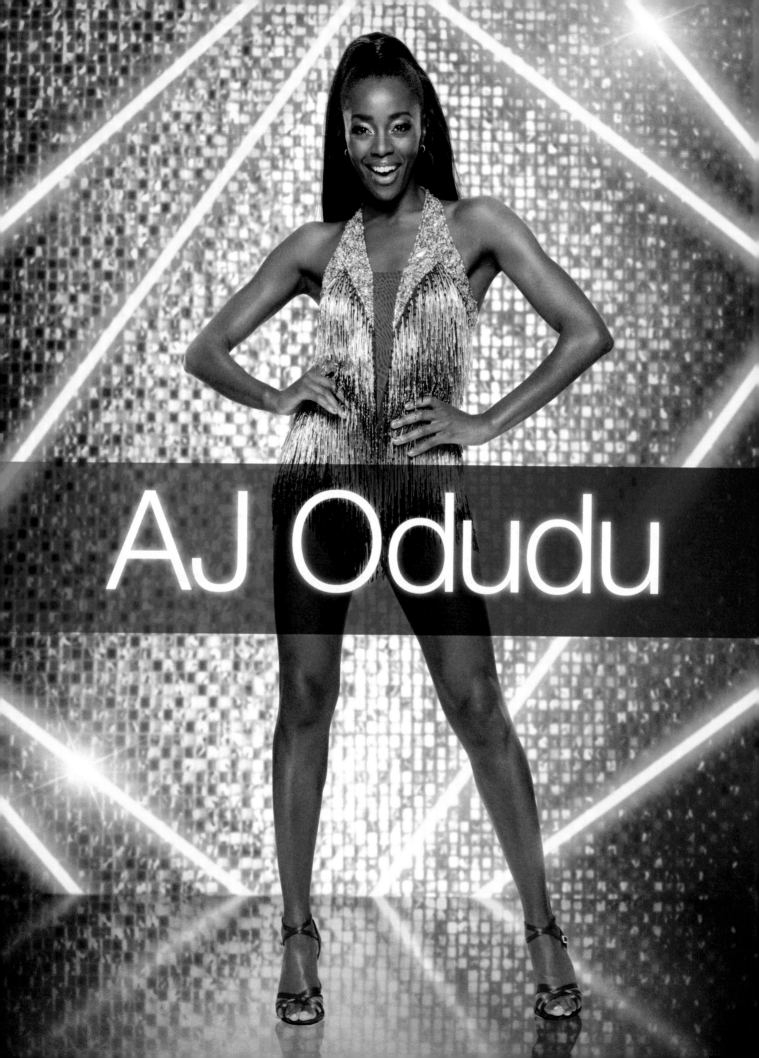

Signing up for *Strictly* was a dream come true for AJ Odudu, and her mum Florence – a *Strictly* superfan – was even more excited.

'My mum is obsessed,' AJ says. 'She has been a fan for years and years and we always watched it together. We even have *Strictly* parties, go on *Strictly* forums and watch it together over the telephone when we're not in the same household.

'She's so excited, but she's really nervous. Hilariously, the other night she said, "I can't wait to come and see the launch show and settle my nerves." I'm thinking, "Mum! *Your* nerves! What about mine?" But she feels a real part of it because it's her baby girl. She's buzzing.'

Born in Blackburn, AJ began her broadcasting career as a radio reporter before fronting *Big Brother's Bit on the Side* with Rylan Clark-Neal and Emma Willis. Although she has presented music shows in the past, AJ says she has no dance background.

'My dance experience amounts to absolutely zero, not even after-school clubs,' she says. 'There was a revolving dance floor in Preston when I was growing up and the sticky dance floors of Blackburn Town Centre, back in the day. I've been on those doing "Oops Upside Your Head" and all of that, but I am a complete novice. I'm definitely one of those people who thinks I can dance when I've had a couple of drinks, like everyone, so let's just see what happens.'

A keen runner, AJ's fitness level will help her with the routines, but she believes she might have to work on her flexibility.

'People assume because I'm athletic and into fitness, I'm good to go but I can't bend and I can't point my toes,' she says. 'I think the hold position for all the ballroom dances will be difficult, so I've been doing some push-ups before bed.'

A huge fan of the sparkles and sequins, AJ says her first wardrobe fitting was an 'absolute dream come true'.

'Imagine a custom-made, sparkly outfit that just fits you like a glove,' she says. 'The whole team are incredible and everyone is on their A-game times a million. It's been such a treat and I feel incredibly lucky.'

While AJ, 33, has her eye on the prize, she believes the other celebrities will give her a run for her money.

'They're all stiff competition,' she says. 'Adam Peaty is an Olympian – that is pretty big competition – and Ugo Monye has a lot of muscles: abs on abs. Sara Davies takes notes in meetings, then scans them, downloads them, makes them a PDF and puts them in our social-media chat. This is why she's an absolute boss. But everyone's just amazing, really likeable and fun.'

Musically, AJ wants to dance to her mum's favourites – Justin Bieber and Rag 'n' Bone Man – as well as her own top tune, Tina Turner's 'Proud Mary'.

'I think my mum will be looking forward to seeing me in the upbeat, feel-good dances she loves, like the Charleston and the Jive,' she adds. 'But also, the Paso Doble – hot, sexy, fierce – she'd love to see me in that light, too.'

While the judges have nothing to fear from AJ herself, she thinks her mum will be fighting her corner.

'Through my experience as a TV presenter, I'm able to take critique and then learn from it. This is an amazing show, with an unbelievable line-up of judges who know their stuff inside out. I just want to listen and learn.

'My mum, on the other hand, is very protective and she only wants to hear good stuff about me. But she knows the spirit of the show, so I'm sure she'll behave herself!'

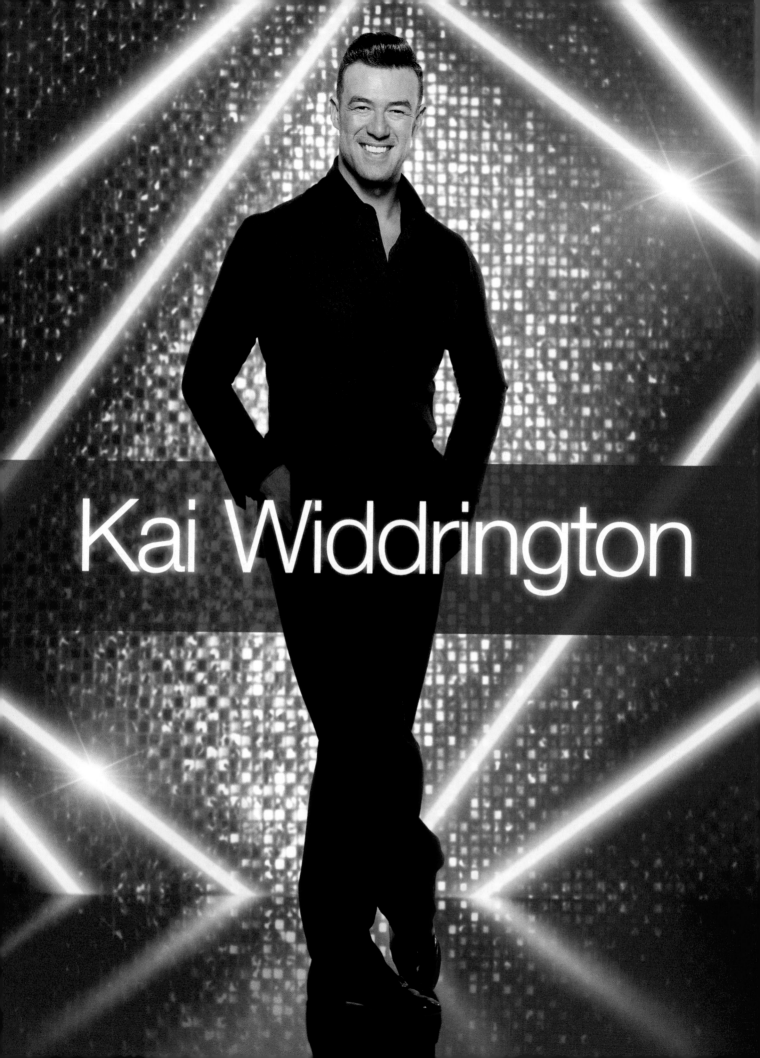

Kai Widdrington

New recruit Kai Widdrington is excited to be joining the *Strictly* professionals after four years on the Irish show *Dancing with the Stars.*

Paired with presenter AJ Odudu, he's looking forward to sharing a journey of discovery together.

'I'm excited to be here and it gets more real every time I go to the studio,' he says. 'I was so happy to be paired with AJ. It's a first for both of us, so we're very excited to embark on this journey together.

'After two days in rehearsal, we're getting on like a house on fire and sharing good banter.'

So far, when it comes to the dance moves, Kai likes what he sees.

'AJ is really capable,' he says. 'There's lots of training to be done, but, at the end of the day, it boils down to the hours you put in. She's more than capable of doing well in this competition and I'm confident I can get her to a good standard. That's my job. The possibilities are endless, and I can't wait to get started.'

The British dancer has already been mulling over some ideas and says AJ has potential in both Latin and ballroom.

'AJ says she prefers the Latin stuff, but she's got lovely long legs that can glide around the floor, a beautiful posture and a long, elegant neck, so I think she's going to be good at ballroom, too. People are often more scared of the Latin, so if she's confident in that, I think we're onto a winner!'

Kai is also convinced his new dance student will work her socks off in the rehearsal room.

'She loves a good chat, but she told me that when it comes down to it, she will definitely put the work in. That's the most important thing for me to hear,' he explains. 'But you need a good balance, and you can't take it too seriously or you won't enjoy it. The celebrities only get to do it once in their life, so you want them to ultimately leave this experience with nothing but positive things to say. I want her to have the best time, but I also want her to leave this competition, whether it's in the Final or week 2, knowing that she's done everything that she could to stay in.'

The son of a professional footballer, Southampton-born Kai almost followed in his dad's footsteps, but at nine he chose to swap football for Botafogos and take up dance. By the time he was 14, he'd become the 2010 World Junior Latin American Champion. At 16, Kai reached the Final of the sixth series of *Britain's Got Talent* and he returned two years later with a ballroom dance group, which also featured Neil and Katya Jones. As a professional on *Dancing with the Stars Ireland* he reached the Final twice. Now he's set to make his mark on the UK show.

'Ireland has an amazing version of the show, but *Strictly* is the biggest show on TV,' he says. 'Also, it's amazing to be dancing in my home country. Ireland feels like a second home to me, and it was always special to dance there, but being on *Strictly* means my mum and friends can watch on the telly, which is wonderful.'

'It's been very easy to fit in for me, and the whole team made me feel very welcome,' he says. 'It's been great to do the group dances with so many friends, old and new.'

As the live shows approach, Kai is eager to let partner AJ experience the satisfaction of a great dance performance.

'In Ireland, I always enjoyed seeing my partner's face once they'd completed a dance – watching them, as a non-performer, experience the applause and feel what it's like to complete an amazing performance. I want AJ to enjoy that and, each week, I look forward to creating magical moments she will always remember.'

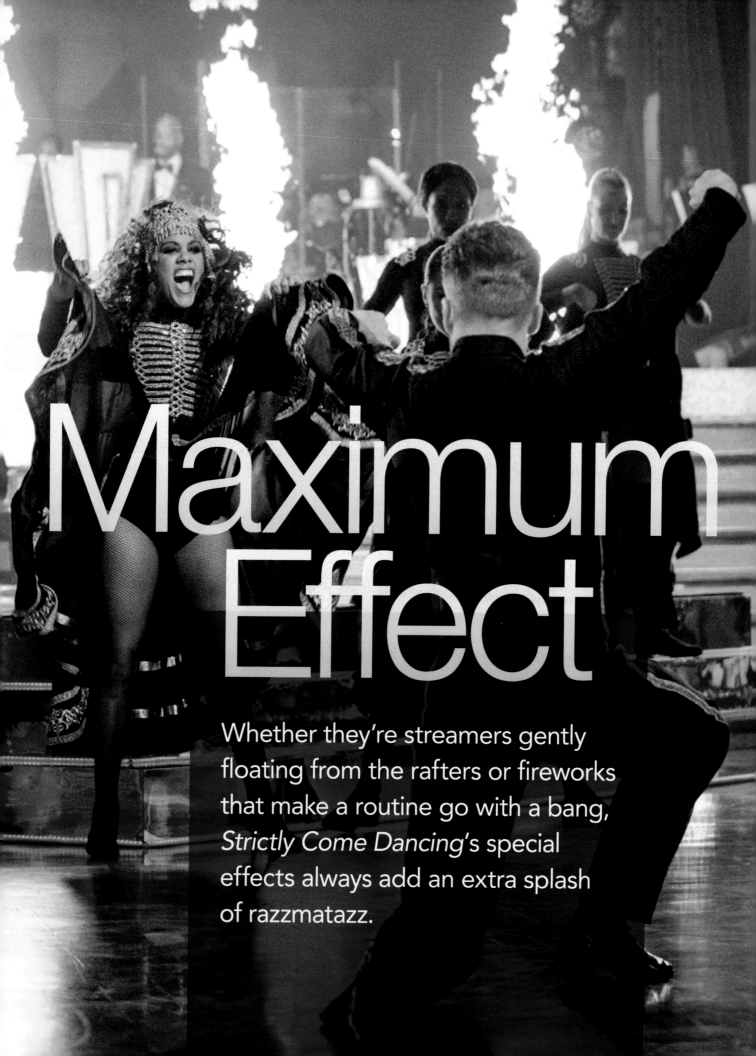

Maximum Effect

Whether they're streamers gently floating from the rafters or fireworks that make a routine go with a bang, *Strictly Come Dancing*'s special effects always add an extra splash of razzmatazz.

From low smoke shrouding a Halloween grave scene to flame throwers and sparkly confetti, the five-strong SFX team, led by Jen Townsend, make the magic happen every Saturday. They can even make it rain.

'We actually flooded the studio for a pro group number to a "Singin' in the Rain"/"Thunder" medley in 2018,' reveals Jen. 'We had a massive rain rig above the dance floor and a tank on the ground. As the professionals danced, we used hoses to flood the tank with hundreds of litres of water, and then we made it rain from above so they could all splash about. It looked absolutely sensational and was one of the best things we've ever done, but it was also nerve-wracking because there are a lot of electrics in a studio, and I had to be very careful not to damage the brand-new dance floor!'

Jen, Director of LiveFX Ltd, also loves to add a little heat to the fiery dances, using flame throwers and towers. 'I love it when we bring flames into the studio, because it looks so atmospheric, especially in some of the Halloween numbers,' she says. 'One of my favourites was Alex Scott's Blackpool Paso, to Beyoncé's "Run the World (Girls)". It was a really empowering number with jets of dancing flames behind her and it was so much fun. Flames give you so much because they light up the studio, but there's also the heat and the audience love it.

'Equally, for me, *Strictly* is all about the confetti in the big group numbers, which looks absolutely stunning. Once we let that confetti go, it always lifts the performance. It's so *Strictly* and so iconic.'

For some of the dances, Jen will find out the details of what is required the week of the show, although for the group numbers, or the more complex visual challenges, she will get an outline of the idea further in advance. As it has to appear seamless on the night, each effect takes careful planning and there are a lot of factors to take into account – not least, safety.

'Some of the effects have an element of risk, so there is a limited area where we can use them because we have to factor in safety distances, particularly with fireworks or flames,' Jen explains. 'We have to protect the dancers, the audience, the judges and presenters and the band, and we need to keep the dance floor as clear as possible.

'On occasion, we have put effects on the dance floor, but that may mean pushing flame bars on during the number, while the cameras are filming the couple at the far end, then lighting them at the end. So it has to be well choreographed between us, the set and props department, lighting, camera work and so on.'

At Friday rehearsals, Jen is on the studio floor, working out exactly how the special effects will work for each dance, where the dancers will move on the floor and when the cue for the release of confetti or the flash of a firework will be.

'If there is a massive flare on the lights at the same time as a pyrotechnic, the audience won't see it, so we work as a real team,' she says. 'I'll talk to Dave Bishop, the Lighting Designer, and tell him when we want to let it off, and he might ask us to do it at a different point, to get the full effect. At the same time, we're working with the dancers, with Creative Director Jason Gilkison and Series Director Nikki Parsons, who is brilliant at hitting those wide shots so the viewers at home can see the pyro and the dance in all their glory.'

Jen also works with costume and make-up to make sure every dancer is safe.

'Bill Bailey had a pyrotechnic guitar for his series 18 showdance, so we made sure he wore leather, which is very protective,' she explains. 'Also, if you've got a floaty costume with chiffon and feathers, you don't want it near a flame unit.'

Although the details are meticulously planned in advance, the team are well prepared for last-minute additions.

and sprinkle confetti while they walk up and down. They have to be fit, because it often means running up five flights of stairs to get to the roof, and they have to be very quiet because they are walking above the dance floor.'

As the walkway is around 18 metres high, the confetti has to be dropped 15 seconds before it needs to be seen below, to give it time to fall.

'At Friday rehearsals, Nikki might say, "Can we pop a pyro at the end of that?" or a dancer wants a routine to end with a flourish, so we have a stock of pyrotechnics, confetti, streamers and smoke on site at the studios. We can look at what lighting are doing and the screens behind and pick something out to add to that performance and the storeroom means we can act quickly.'

Even with the finesses ironed out on a Friday, Jen has to think on her feet during the live show.

'On Saturday night, the adrenaline is pumping and the couples are really going for it, so they might dance slightly differently to in rehearsals,' says Jen. 'We're constantly watching them and making split-second decisions as to whether it's safe to go ahead, because if they fly around the dance floor even a metre further out than they did in rehearsals, it might make all the difference.'

While Jen's arsenal includes CO_2 cannons, which fire confetti and streamers up into the air, there are some jobs that have to be done manually – and at dizzying heights.

'The confetti cannons are great for the big party dances, but for a gentle waltz or a beautiful ballroom dance we don't want a rush of confetti, just a gentle drop of petals or snowflakes. At Elstree Studios, there's a walkway up in the roof, above all the lighting rigs, which crosses the dance floor downstage of the judges, and another just in front of the band. Our team stand up there

The effects team also have to make sure their radios are securely tied to their belts and there's nothing in their pockets that could fall out, so they don't drop a clanger.

The team's remit is not just staging the dazzling effects, but also clearing up quickly between dances, without being caught on camera, which they carry out with ninja-like skill.

'When the dance finishes and the couple go over to the judges, we move in with big mops and we're sweeping up three or four metres away from them, on the dance floor,' says Jen. 'We sneak in and out behind the cameras, keeping out of the shots, and as soon as they've been critiqued by the last judge, we know they are going to run up the stairs to Claudia's area so we run off the dance floor. While they're up with Claudia, we run back on again, taking care not to get in the way of the judges during scoring. All the time, Nikki is calling the shots from the gallery and she'll say, "Jen, we're coming to the judges," so we drop back or lie on the floor, and they take the shot above our heads. The choreography doesn't just happen on the dance floor – it happens with us before and after.

'After one dance in Blackpool, where Claudia's area is not elevated, we were collecting the streamers by swimming along the floor, on our tummies, because we couldn't stand up without being seen, and Gethin Jones tweeted a video of it, which was fun. It's one of the most entertaining

parts of the job, because you're trying to keep out of the way, but the live audience is looking at us thinking, "What are you doing? Surely you can be seen!"'

Among the many changes in recent years is a move towards sustainable products. The sparkly metallic confetti, for example, was once made from a polyester-based product, but since the show went plastic-free a few years ago, all confetti and streamers are made from biodegradable paper.

Another big difference is the number of dances that now use some special effects, with an average of 75 per cent of the couple dances and every group number benefitting from that extra razzle-dazzle.

'In the first year, the only special effects were at the winning moment of the Final, but now it is the majority of the dances,' says Jen. 'The effects we can achieve have got bigger, the stage is bigger, the studio's bigger and the production values are so high. With *Strictly*, the sparklier the better and the audience love the razzmatazz. Whenever we do a pyrotechnic, for example, the live audience scream – so it all adds to the atmosphere in the studio as well as looking amazing on screen.'

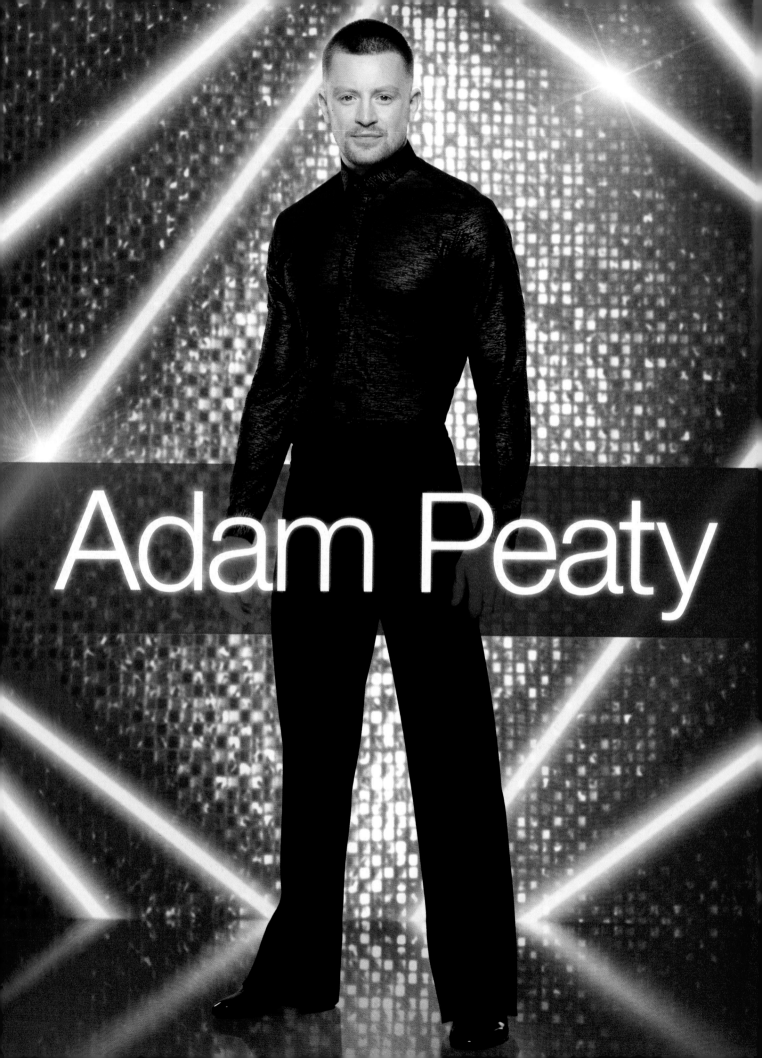

Fresh from his triumph at the Tokyo Olympics, where he picked up two gold medals for Team GB, swimmer Adam Peaty is ready to try out his moves on dry land. And he's hoping to add to his heaving trophy cabinet with the famous glitterball.

'I wanted to take a bit of time away from swimming, because it's been my whole life for the last eight or nine years,' he says. 'I'm not sure if my swimming skills will help me on the dance floor. In fact, they'll probably be a hindrance, because I'm used to being in the water and not being on land, working against gravity. But hopefully my hips are going to be quite fluid.'

As an Olympian, Adam is incredibly fit and accustomed to a punishing training regime – which will help when it comes to long hours in the rehearsal room. But he's having a well-earned rest before strapping on his dancing shoes.

'Swimming training is among the hardest, so I'm used to going up and down the pool for four hours and then going to the gym for two hours a day. It's quite tedious, but dancing, with music, will be completely different. I'm guessing it's going to be extremely hard, but I like that. I've trained my mind and body for a long time, so it's about putting the hard work to good use.'

Born in Staffordshire, Adam began competing at 12. In 2016 he won his first Olympic gold in Rio de Janeiro, and this summer he became the first British swimmer to retain the medal, at the delayed Tokyo Games.

Although he's never had dance lessons, Adam rates himself as an enthusiastic amateur on the floor – at least at weddings and parties.

'I am a party dancer and I love getting those hips moving,' he says. 'I guess I would rate my dancing, but when it comes to ballroom and Latin, it's a very different scenario. I've always liked ballroom and I like watching it, especially on TV. I'm nervous about the Latin dances because they're so fluid, but I'm high energy so I'm just going to go for it.'

Adam has eclectic music taste and has been gathering a few ideas for his *Strictly* routines ahead of the series.

'Max Richter is my favourite composer and I love classical music,' he says. 'But if I'm in a club or a bar, it's obviously dance or drum and bass that I dance to, so, again, it's high energy. I've got my own playlist ready to go, but it changes as to what kind of day it is and who I'm hanging around with. I'm also a massive fan of musicals, so I hope I make it to Musicals Week.'

As a sportsman, Adam is used to constructive criticism, but he's hoping for high scores from the judges.

'I can take criticism, but if I think it's a good dance, I've put my heart and soul into it and hours and hours of training, then I get a three or four, I'm not going to be happy,' he jokes.

Whatever the competition throws at him, the 26-year-old has vowed to keep laughing – and bringing some humour into his routine.

'I don't take life too seriously and when training is tough I rely on my humour and my ability to smile in the face of adversity,' he says. 'That's my personality and I hope that can come through in some of the dances. As long as the sun rises, we've got another opportunity to have a laugh.'

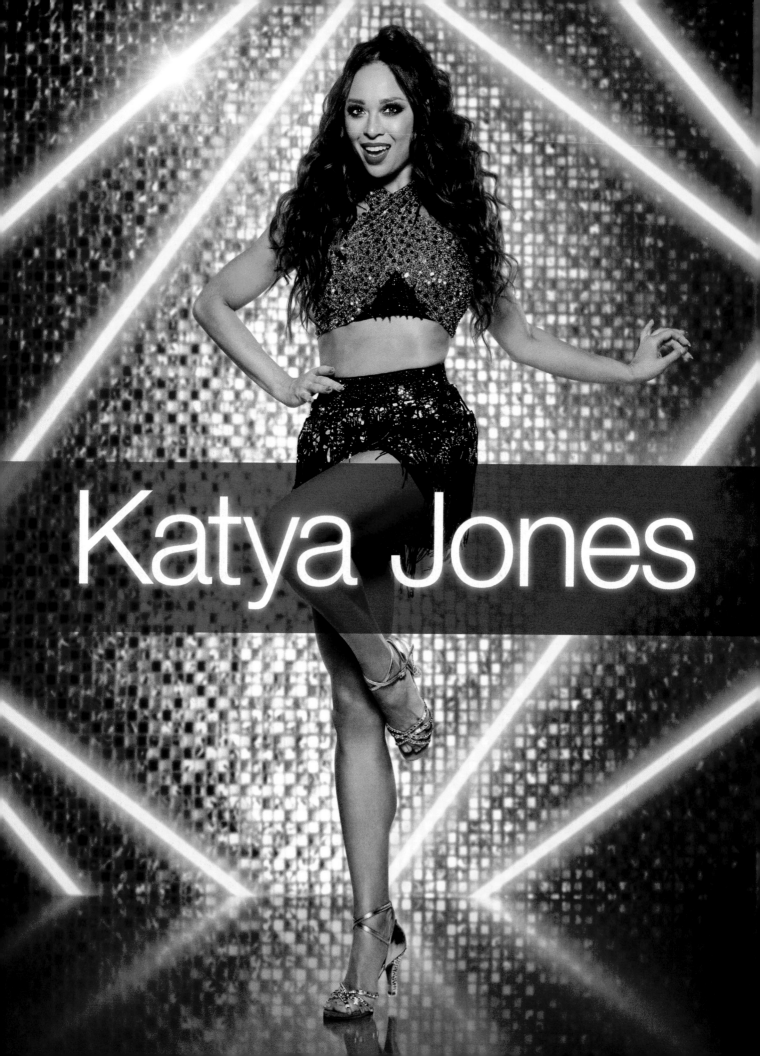

Katya Jones

Former champ Katya Jones has been paired with Olympic gold medallist Adam Peaty for this year's contest, and they are already getting on swimmingly.

'We met at the Aquatics Centre in the Olympic Village in East London, and he swam up to me, got out of the pool and gave me a massive hug,' she says.

'Adam is a really nice guy, willing to work hard, with great energy. But he is up for a laugh as well. As a top-level athlete, he's focused 365 days a year. So while this is obviously a challenge, and out of his comfort zone, he wants to have a fun time as well. He's not scared to show his silly side and I love that!'

Having just returned from Tokyo with a haul of three medals, the Team GB swimmer is at the peak of physical fitness, and Katya is planning to work him hard.

'Adam's used to being trained really hard and I'm kind of known for being quite tough, so I think there will be a meeting of minds there,' she says. 'When we were paired, I told him, "Get ready for 12-hour days!" and he was a bit surprised, but he's up for it. He's in great shape and will have stamina. As a swimmer he also has to be quite flexible and aware of his body, so that will help, and he has a really positive attitude, so it's very exciting.'

As Adam has had a triumphant year in his sport, Katya hints that there may be some reference to his achievements in her choreography but says viewers will have to wait and see.

'Adam wants to do a Waltz to classical music,' she says. 'But other than that, I don't yet know. When we get into the rehearsal room is when I can get the gist of what my celebrity is like as a student and what their movement is like, and then I start building from that rather than getting ideas in my head that may not suit them. The first thing we'll do is throw some shapes around, see how he reacts to teaching, and from there we will come up with some fun stuff.'

Born in Saint Petersburg, Katya has been dancing since she was six, and is three-time World Amateur Latin Champion. In 2015, she won the World Professional Latin Showdance Championship and she is also the four-time undefeated British National Professional Champion. She joined *Strictly* in series 14 and lifted the glitterball with actor Joe McFadden the following year. In series 18 she danced with boxer Nicola Adams as part of *Strictly*'s first same-sex couple.

'No matter how short our journey was, Nicola's message was delivered, and that's all that matters,' she says.

The talented choreographer says that dancing in an all-female partnership opened new possibilities for her.

'It's really creative and interesting because we can switch the lead and follow rules within the routine, so I went from being just the follower to leading certain parts, which was exciting.'

As she plunges into the deep end with her new celebrity partner, Katya is hoping he'll come away with a passion for movement on dry land.

'Teaching my celebrity and seeing the improvement is my favourite part,' she says. 'Hopefully, the show will allow people to see that while he's an Olympian swimmer, he is focused and strong-minded – he's up for a new challenge. My aim is for him to fall in love with dancing and inspire everybody to take on new challenges and not be afraid.'

Jowita Przystał

Although she's new to the professional team, Jowita Przystał may already be familiar to *Strictly* viewers.

She and partner Michael Danilczuk performed on the results show after winning *The Greatest Dancer* in 2020, but her ultimate dream has always been to join the show.

'I was at home eating my breakfast when I got the call offering me the job and I just couldn't believe it,' she says. 'Michael started screaming. I started to cry and then said, "Are you joking?" I feel so blessed and happy, and I just can't wait to be on the live shows every Saturday.'

Born in Poland, Jowita started dancing at six, trying out cheerleading, ballet and jazz before moving into ballroom and Latin at 12.

'My mum was in love with ballroom, but I didn't want to dance with a boy!' she laughs. 'I'm very petite and as a child I was little, so my mum imagined me in the beautiful dresses with the rhinestones. So when I was 12 I said I would try it and tell her how I feel, and I just fell in love in the first class. Ballroom has been the biggest love of my life since.'

Jowita went on to become Polish Open Latin Champion. Before joining *Strictly* she had already been mentored by Oti on *The Greatest Dancer*, but she says all the professionals made her feel welcome.

'Oti was very excited when I was offered *Strictly* and I get so much support and help from her,' she says. 'I know I can count on her and she's always there for me as a great friend and a great dancer. The rest of the team is amazing. Every one of them was so warm and welcoming, and made us feel like we weren't new to the team at all, like we have been part of the family for a long time. We had an amazing time in the group dances and I just can't wait for more.'

Having encouraged her onto the dance floor, Jowita's mum is thrilled to see her land her dream job on the show.

'I'm an only child and my parents worked hard when I was growing up so that I could dance,' she says. 'They are both so proud of me and I'm hoping they will be able to come and see me dance live on the show this year.'

Bubbling with excitement, Jowita, 26, says she can't narrow down what she is looking forward to most about the coming series.

'I'm excited for everything,' she says. 'Just to be there in the studio. I love live music so whenever I hear the band playing, my heart melts, my legs bend and I want to dance.

'The group numbers are going to be fantastic, full of surprises, because they are different from anything they've done before. Creating them was such a beautiful experience and every one of the numbers is so special, so I can't wait to see them.

'Also, even though it is a competition, I feel like we are such a family. Every time we are together it is like a big festival and I just love being around these people.'

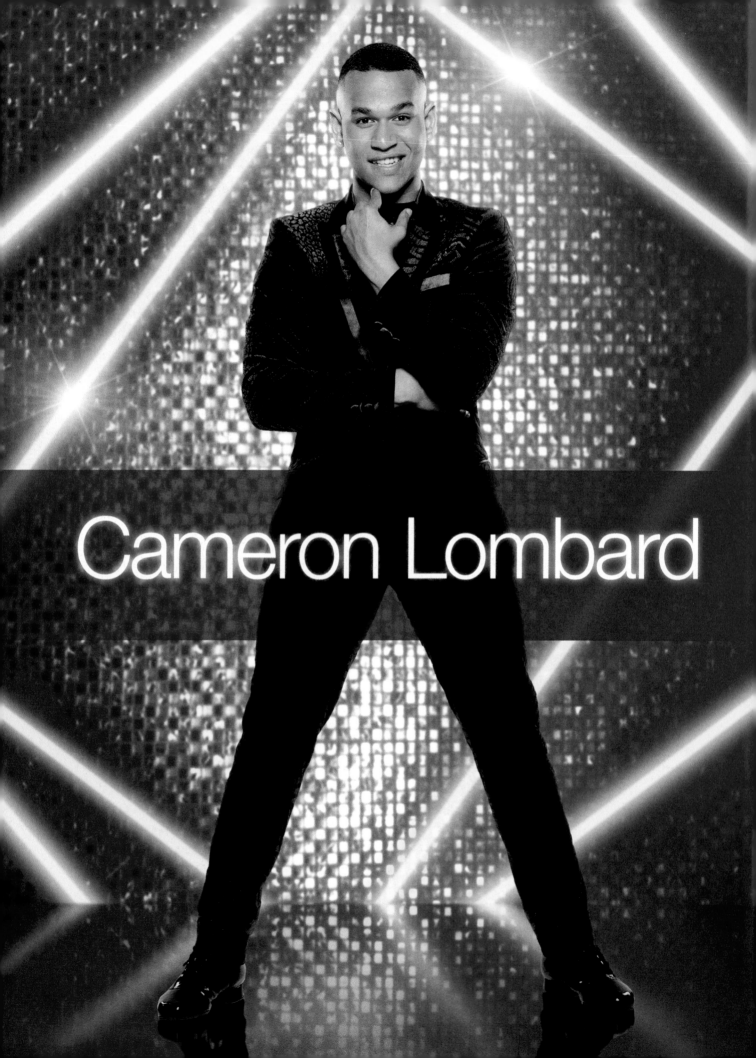

Cameron Lombard

New pro Cameron Lombard is following in the footsteps of fellow South Africans Oti Mabuse and Johannes Radebe and says both were his inspiration as a junior dancer.

'When I was competing, at the age of ten, Motsi was already an international champion, Oti was South African Champion and Johannes was in the adult championship section, so I've always looked up to them,' he says. 'Both Oti and Johannes have given me advice and taken me under their wing. It's such an honour for me to be on the same stage, representing the same country. I'm so overwhelmed and every day it gets a bit more real!'

At 20, Cameron is the youngest pro on the show, and he says his new colleagues have made him feel welcome.

'They have all made me feel at home and their talent is so uplifting, it gives me motivation to do better each time,' he says. 'Obviously, I'm the baby so I take all the advice I can get, but they've treated me really well. The Strictly family is definitely a family that I will hold close to my heart.'

Cameron began dancing at the age of five, in his native Cape Town, after accompanying his older sister to a class at a nearby studio. 'At first I wasn't interested, being five years old, and was running around the studio, but then she was entered into a competition and I saw the way the adult champions moved and the discipline of the sport. As soon as I got home, I said, "Mum, that is exactly the guy I want to be." It's taken off ever since.'

Now reigning South African Latin Champion, Cameron has won 18 national titles across ballroom and Latin during his dance career. In 2019 he represented South Africa at the World Championships.

Although he has moved to London to join Strictly, it's not the first time he's visited as he competed in the UK three times as a child.

'I danced at the Royal Albert Hall in 2010, and my dance teacher sent me to get some crystals for the dresses from Neil Jones and Katya,' he recalls. 'So I met them in the locker room. Who would have thought, ten years later, I'd be sharing the Strictly stage with them!'

'But London already feels like home. There's a certain scent when you first land in London and as soon as I smelt that, I felt like that little boy from all those years ago. I love everything about the UK – the trains, the buses, the environment and, of course, the football. My dad and I are big Manchester United supporters, so hopefully I can experience the football stadiums while I'm here.'

The young dancer will be celebrating his twenty-first birthday in November, and says he is looking forward to celebrating it with his Strictly colleagues.

'I'm here in London on the biggest show in the UK, so what more could I want?' he says. 'I think I'd like to get dressed up and have a lovely supper with people that mean a lot to me, like the new friends that I've met on the show.'

After throwing himself into the group dances, Cameron says his first few weeks were a steep learning curve.

'The group dancing has been awesome,' he says. 'In the beginning, it was quite difficult because my body was able to do the dancing, but my mind was taking in all this knowledge, so I needed to work hard. But it has been amazing, and I can definitely say I stepped up a level. What I'm looking forward to now is gaining more knowledge from this experience because, being the age I am, I'm constantly absorbing information. I'm also excited to be on the BBC and making my family proud and working with these awesome people, because these guys are on a completely different level.'

Luba Mushtuk

Russian dancer Luba Mushtuk is thrilled to be back in the studio with her fellow professionals after eight months apart, and she can't wait to spread some *Strictly* sparkle on a Saturday night.

'Every year, I look forward to the whole magic of this show,' she says. 'Because it is a family and we are all so passionate about what we're doing. Every single one of us puts all of what we have into the show and it's very special to be part of this talented team. We really care for each other, and every season feels like a party. Once we are in our *Strictly* bubble, it feels like home. It's magical.'

Although not dancing with a celebrity this year, Luba will be featured in the group dances and performing with the guest music acts on the results show. And she promises viewers are in for a treat from the pros.

'The group dances this year are incredible,' she says. 'Even when you think they can't get any better than last year, they always do. The routines are insane. The pro dances travel to many different places this year – there's a western number, an Irish-themed number and a brilliant routine where I am painted green – to match my eyes. You'll have to wait and see why!'

Luba was born in Saint Petersburg but moved to Italy at 12 to study dance under legendary teacher Caterina Arzenton. She went on to become four-time winner of the Italian Dance Championship and Italian Open Latin Showdance Champion. She joined the professional dancers in 2018 and, last year, she partnered American Football star Jason Bell.

'I had the best time with Jason and made a friend for life,' she says. 'I absolutely adore the guy and we had so much fun. Every celebrity who comes in needs a very different approach, and it takes the first few days to understand what works best for them. Because he had a coach for so many years, he needed me to be like a coach and quite strict. But he was very good at listening, and even when he was tired he would want to keep repeating the moves until he got it right. He worked really hard.'

Luba has also been helping the four new professionals settle in.

'I think they are having the best time and we are all trying to help them with advice and anything they want to know,' she says. 'But they are all lovely and extremely talented.'

Word Search Answers

V	S	H	E	E	D	L	Z	J	A	B	B	X	U	C
Y	E	L	R	I	H	S	T	R	U	M	B	A	S	S
L	P	N	O	M	T	Q	A	R	C	G	A	R	C	F
E	F	C	O	O	R	B	J	I	V	E	Z	X	L	T
C	F	O	L	L	A	B	P	X	I	L	B	E	A	S
H	E	U	F	K	C	A	R	N	E	W	R	S	D	H
A	D	R	E	W	O	T	P	V	N	E	T	U	O	O
R	A	T	C	X	T	W	E	B	N	R	H	B	F	W
L	E	A	N	C	O	R	R	L	E	O	T	A	R	D
E	X	B	A	O	G	Q	U	E	S	R	O	M	T	A
S	F	Z	D	I	N	D	N	F	E	L	I	B	S	N
T	Z	T	A	S	A	L	S	A	K	F	N	P	A	C
O	C	R	O	U	T	R	L	O	X	Y	E	L	A	E
N	C	E	L	Y	E	L	I	A	B	L	L	I	B	H
T	R	I	P	P	R	C	N	E	I	V	L	I	R	F

Crossword Answers

R¹	Y	L²	A	N³	C	L⁴	A	R	K⁵	N	E	A	L⁶
I		E		E		I			I				U
C		T		W		N			S				B
H⁷	O	S	T	S		D		S⁸	A	M	B	A
A		D		R⁹	Y	A	N					
R¹⁰	O	O	F			H						
D		I		T¹¹	O	M	A¹³	R	C¹⁴	H
	S¹⁵	T	E	P		P¹⁶	U	T		A		P¹⁷
						S			F¹⁸	R	E	E
		S¹⁹		S²⁰	P	I	N		O		R
R²¹	U	M	B	A²²		C		C²³	O	L	I	N
A		I		L		A		O		I		I
N		T		A		L		L		N		C
J²⁴	O	H	A	N	N	E	S	R	A	D	E	B	E

Quiz Answers

1. 2004
2. Darren Gough
3. Jamie Laing
4. Bill Bailey
5. Aliona Vilani
6. Latin – Shirley is known as the Queen of Latin
7. Anton Du Beke
8. Cuba
9. HRVY
10. Nancy Dell'Olio
11. Abbey Clancy
12. Aston Merrygold
13. Television Centre
14. The Jive
15. 2018